FALLEN GIANTS

THE COMBAT DEBUT OF THE T-35A TANK

FRANCIS PULHAM

Fonthill Media Language Policy

Fonthill Media publishes in the international English language market. One language edition is published worldwide. As there are minor differences in spelling and presentation, especially with regard to American English and British English, a policy is necessary to define which form of English to use. The Fonthill Policy is to use the form of English native to the author. Francis Pulham was born and educated in Brighton, UK and therefore British English has been adopted in this publication.

Fonthill Media Limited
Fonthill Media LLC
www.fonthillmedia.com
office@fonthillmedia.com

First published in the United Kingdom and the United States of America 2017

British Library Cataloguing in Publication Data:
A catalogue record for this book is available from the British Library

Copyright © Francis Pulham 2017

ISBN 978-1-78155-626-9

The right of Francis Pulham to be identified as the author of this work has been asserted by him in accordance with the Copyright, Designs and Patents Act 1988.

All rights reserved. No part of this publication may be reproduced, stored in a retrieval system or transmitted in any form or by any means, electronic, mechanical, photocopying, recording or otherwise, without prior permission in writing from Fonthill Media Limited

Typeset in 10.5pt on 13pt Minion Pro
Printed and bound by CPI Group (UK) Ltd, Croydon, CR0 4YY

Acknowledgements

Other books about the T-35A have covered its design, production, and aspects of its career in great detail; however, an annotated guide of the T-35A in the field has never been published as a book before. This book would not have been made without the help from Sergey Lotarev (photographs and information); Vladimir Nemeshin (photographs); Maxim Kolomiets (photographs); John Prigent (photographs); Craig Moore (photographs); Will Kerrs (editor and co-author); Stan Lucian (editor); Jonathan Paul Liautrakul (art); and David Bocquelet (art: tanks-encyclopedia.com).

This publication was partly funded by the community though Kickstarter. In total, £573 was raised to help with the resource gathering and art that was used in this book. The following backers helped greatly with this book:

£25 Backers
Craig Moore.

£30 Backers
Stan Lucian and Will Kerrs.

£50 Backers
Lauren Child, Alex Smith, Duane Warnecke, Lorenzo Dutto, John Whoodhouse, Jeff Pulham, Tony Makinder, Anthony Perkins, Lawrance Ambrose, and Andery Fi.

Without the generous backing from these people, this book would be shorter, lower quality, and less professional. A massive thank you to all those who pledged to make this book a reality.

Contents

Acknowledgements   3
Introduction   7

1. The History of the T-35A Tank   9
2. The Battle of Brody and the Battle at Verba   18
3. The Combat Debut of the T-35A Tank in Photos   25
4. Art of the T-35A   125
5. Tanks that Served Alongside T-35 Tanks   132
6. Reviewing the Performance of the T-35A   139

Sources and Further Reading   144

Introduction

This publication is attempting something never done before in English, and follows on from the research of Sergey Lotarev. Using the surviving records of the chassis numbers of the tanks that were manufactured and the surviving war records of the losses of the 67th and 68th Tank Regiments, then cross-referencing these with the photographs that German soldiers took during the war with modern locations in Ukraine, the T-35s have been categorised into chassis numbers to the full extent of available information.

The identification process of a tank does use an element of speculation; however, this is absolutely necessary as specifics are often lost to time. The first step towards identification of a T-35 in a photograph is to compare it to other tanks. Using this simple method, the tanks can be divided into different categories. These include single-hatched tanks, tanks with a P-40 AA mount, and conical tanks. From here, one can use the objects in the picture or any text on the reverse to try to find a location, if there are any of these details. If this is successful, it is then possible to use the table of tank losses to identify a chassis number.

An example of this would be T-35 chassis number 183-3. Photographic evidence of the tank shows it in a small urban area, and some photographs have a church in them. Sometimes, a photo will have a location written on the back; this is one of the most useful pieces of information. Using Google Maps and image searches, one can find the location and verify if this is indeed the correct location. If it is not the correct location, normally the soldier will be off by only one or two villages. The location of 183-3 is the town of Bilyi Kamin. Using this information, one can look at the documentation of the losses to find if any tanks were lost near or at that location. The 183-3 is located correctly in the documentation; however, a tank like 148-25 is listed as the next village along to the one they were actually lost in. It was only through using and cross-referencing these different location techniques that tanks can be confirmed as a certain chassis number.

1

The History of the T-35A Tank

The T-35A tank is one of history's strangest tanks, often seen crawling across Soviet inter-war parade squares. This tank grabbed the hearts, souls, and imaginations of the Soviet people and foreign military *attachés* alike. It was one of the many proud achievements of Soviet industrialisation; its image appeared on posters, films, and even medals and awards. However, the grandeur was not to last.

With storms brewing over Europe in the latter half of the 1930s, many nations began to modernise and expand their tank arsenals. As a consequence, the T-35A very quickly found itself outclassed by other machines. However, despite this, these tanks found themselves fighting against the German Army's advance across Russia in 1941. Many Wehrmacht soldiers encountered these giant relics from better days, and they certainly attracted much enthusiastic attention. However, as the war pressed on, the T-35A was soon forgotten as a strange oddity from the east. Only in recent years has the tank gained attention for being a lost relic rediscovered.

Design and Development

The T-35 tank was commissioned after the cancellation of the TG tank project in 1931. The TG tank was a joint German-Soviet design for a heavy tank, with two turret layers bristling with armaments. The RKKA (Workers' and Peasants' Red Army) dismissed the TG project, and the designer, the German-born Ernst Grotte, moved back to Germany to continue his career in tank building. The RKKA concluded that the vehicle had too many flaws, and pursued a new, multi-turret tank which would eventually become the T-35. Some will claim that the T-35 was inspired by the A1E1 Independent tank, but Soviet-era sources claim the A1E1 had no influence on the design, despite Soviet knowledge of the vehicle.

A new heavy tank prototype was designed in early 1932, designated 'T-35-1'. It was produced at the Kharkiv Locomotive Factory (KhPZ). This first prototype had six pairs of road wheels arranged with two pairs of road wheels per bogie. Each bogie was fitted with coiled spring suspension comprised of two pairs of springs. All of the sub-turrets of the prototype were of the same design and shape—two had 37-mm PS-2 guns, and the other two had DT-29 machine guns. When facing forward and aft of the tank, the 37-mm turrets were on the right, while the machine gun turrets were on the left. The main turret was fitted with a 76.2-mm PS-3 gun. It was welded with a distinctive curved roof and rested on an armoured pedestal.

The tank had two armoured skirts on either side to protect the suspension; however, rather foolishly, the skirts of the first prototype had no access ports, and there was no way to access the suspension without pulling the skirts apart. The tank was powered by the M-17L aircraft engine, with the drive wheel at the rear. The tracks ran over the top of six return rollers that were almost two metres above the ground. This prototype was evaluated in mid-1932 before a second prototype was ordered.

The second prototype was outwardly similar, with the exception of the addition of access ports in the skirts. These were square shaped and gave all important access to the bogies for maintenance. In addition, the main turret relinquished the round roof. Accordingly, this prototype was called the 'T-35-2'.

These T-35 prototypes were both evaluated but were not accepted for Red Army service. However, a radically changed design was accepted; it was called the T-35A. 'T-35A' is the western term for the tank. The German army technical records, which were issued to crews, gave letters to the designations of enemy tanks. Technically, all T-35s of all types and designs were simply T-35s in the USSR. However, for the purposes of this book, T-35s with cylindrical turrets will be called T-35A and conical turreted tanks will be called T-35.

The T-35-1 and T-35-2 prototypes at Palace Square in Leningrad. Similarities with the production tank include the turret layout and basic crew position; however, many differences include a shorter chassis, smaller turrets, two fewer bogies, and smaller calibre guns. The T-35-1 had a curved roof, whereas the T-35-2 had a flat roof.

The new tank was longer, which required the addition of an extra bogie. The turrets were also redesigned. The 45-mm gun turrets were now round with room for two crew to operate a more potent K-20 gun. The machine gun turrets were very similar to the secondary turrets on the T-28 medium tank. These turrets were all produced in Leningrad.

The exhausts were moved from the fenders to the main body of the tank. This was done in order to protect the exhaust from damage. Finally, the main turret was now elliptical. It was identical to the main turret of the new T-28 tank. It featured a 76.2-mm KT-28 gun, an electrically powered turret traverse system, and complex electronics. In addition, a 71-KT-1 radio with distinctive 'clothes line' antenna was added.

Description of the T-35

The T-35 tank was 9.72 metres (31.8 feet) long by 3.2 metres (10.4 feet) wide by 3.43 metres (11.2 feet) high, and weighed 54 metric tons. The tank was powered by the M-17L aero engine, which had an output of 580 hp. The tank could travel up to 28 km/h on roads and 14 km/h off road. The hull was manufactured from plates that were 20 mm thick on the sides, 10 mm on the roof and floor, and 30 mm on the glacis and nose. The hull sides had four hard points for the bogies of the tank, and a drive wheel at the rear.

The running gear consisted of four bogies. Each bogie was made up of four coiled spring suspension arms in two pairs, with two pairs of road wheels in between them. There was a drive wheel at the rear of the tank, and six return rollers, which were the same as the T-28's road wheels. The track consisted of 135 links that were 526 mm in width.

In between the bogies were supporting brackets that attach to a skirt of metal that was on the exterior of the hull. These were made from five plates. Each plate was 10 mm thick and attached to the bogie and the return roller. This skirt was attached to a frame on the inside, and individual skirt parts could be removed. The skirt was attached to the fender, which ran from the front of the tank to the rear of the tank and was where all of the equipment for the tank was stowed.

The engine deck consisted of a central hatch to access the engine, with two air intakes for the radiators either side of the engine access hatch. Behind this was the exhaust, which was originally an exterior exhaust with an armoured cover for the front and sides. The rear of the tank sloped downwards, where a huge fan was situated. This fan had a cover, which was attached to the tank by hinges, and had vertical slats on it to allow for air flow. Below this were two rear transmission hatches.

The tank had five turrets in the forward two-thirds of the tank. These were arranged around a central turret pedestal. In front and behind were two turrets—a 45-mm turret with a MG turret to the 45-mm gun turrets on the left. The MG turrets were redesigned turrets from the T-28 tank and were equipped with a ball mounted DT-29 machine gun. This turret had a single hatch and a single vision port to the left.

The 45-mm gun turret was round, with a 45-mm K-20 gun facing forwards. The armour was 20 mm thick, and on the turret interior walls was 45-mm gun ammunition. Three racks were carried—one between the two vision ports on the right, one against the rear wall of the turret, and one on the right wall. The rear ammunition rack could be removed, exposing a door at the rear of the turret that allowed for gun removal and maintenance. A magazine rack was also carried in this turret with enough space for seven magazines of thirty rounds. This turret had a crew of two men—a gunner and a loader. The gunner was also equipped with a TP-1 periscope. The turret roof also had a smoke extractor and two hatches for the crew.

The main turret sat on a pedestal that elevated it above the 45-mm gun turrets. The main turret was elliptical in shape, with a slightly offset KT-28 76.2-mm gun. To the gun's right was a cheek-mounted DT-29 machine gun in a ball mount. To the left of the gun was the turret traverse mechanism. The turret was connected to a rotating floor plate by five arms. On the rotating turret floor were two seats for the gunner and the loader, with stowage for six 76-mm rounds underneath each seat. Directly underneath the KT-28 gun was an ammunition rack for DT-29 machine gun ammunition. On the rear arm that connected the turret to the rotating turret floor was a folding seat for the commander.

The turret roof was equipped with two TP-1 periscopes for the gunner and the loader. The first tanks were issued with turrets with a single square turret hatch for the crew. Whereas, the later tanks were issued with a second hatch for the loader and a P-40 AA mount for the commander and gunner hatch. The turret roof had a pressed star between the two periscopes. The roof top also had small spring stoppers for the main hatches.

The walls of the pedestals were equipped with ammunition racks for the 76.2-mm ammunition, and 7.62-mm DT-29 machine gun ammunition. Within the turret and pedestal was a 71-TK-1 radio set, and the tanks were all issued with clothes line antennae. Ninety-six rounds of 76.2-mm ammunition was carried, and 226 rounds of 45-mm ammunition was carried. In addition, 10,080 rounds of DT-29 ammunition was carried in 380 magazines. The rear of the main turret also has a port for a DT-29 machine gun; however, no ball mount was issued until production of conical T-35s began.

The tank had a crew of ten—three crew in the main turret (commander, gunner, and loader), two crew in the 45-mm gun turrets (gunner, loader), one crewman in each 45-mm gun turret, and the driver.

There was a production issue in 1936 that meant a batch of hulls were issued with 23-mm plates; however, it was not until 1938 that the thickness of the tanks armour was increased. The turret armour was increased to 25 mm, and the nose glacis armour was redesigned to be 80 mm thick. Conical tanks also had a redesigned skirt with inspection ports. These ports were originally at a 40-degree angle; however, in the last four tanks, the skirts access ports were manufactured with square ports.

Changes to production

Production started in 1934, and by 1939, fifty-nine vehicles were produced, although most statistics include the two prototypes, increasing the number to sixty-one tanks (see Table 1).

Throughout production, improvements were constantly being made. For example, in 1934, the turret antenna was changed from having six to eight connecting arms. This was due to the antenna often breaking. The turret was also given an additional strip of armour which was used to hide and strengthen seams.

However, in 1936, the first major changes occurred. The main single turret hatch was replaced with two hatches and a P-40 anti-aircraft gun mount was added. At about this time, the exhaust was moved under the armour of the tank, and two exhaust pipes now protruded from the tank. Additionally, the thickness of the armour was increased on the machine gun turrets. The driver's hatch was redesigned to reach the top of the glacis plate.

Each tank had a chassis number, and these were made in batches, often not exceeding five tanks. The batch number was always three numbers, a hyphen, then one or two numbers. Chassis numbers starting with 148, 339, 288, 220, 228, 183, and 537 all had a single-turret hatch (a total of thirty-one tanks), while chassis numbers 715, 0197, 217, 196, 988, and 0200 all had P-40 AA mounts (a total of nineteen tanks).

The next set of major changes in production occurred in 1938. The rear part of the side skirt was removed to prevent mud build up around the drive wheel, something that often caused major problems with the track during manoeuvres. The skirts were now fitted with inspection ports, which were triangular. Also, the smoke generators were made to be homogeneous with the sub turret structure. This was applied to chassis numbers 196-94 and 196-95. After twelve more tanks were produced to the previous specification, production modernised to the new standard.

In 1938, the tanks turrets were changed drastically to a more distinctive conical shape to improve the effective thickness of the armour and increase the longevity of the tank as its lifespan was already in question. The new hull, with inspection ports in the skirts, was re-equipped, previously being used on the experimental hulls 196-94 and 196-95. The conical turreted tanks were not issued clothes line antennae after 234-42, and a simple rod antenna was implemented. The final tanks produced were modified further; the smoke generator armour was angled, and the inspection ports were made square.

Two T-35s crawl across the parade square. These two tanks have a single turret hatch and eight antenna arms. Notice the pre-war paint scheme and the divisional markings on the hull.

While the production runs differed, tanks were often taken back to factories and upgraded further. For example, a great majority of tanks had the old exhaust pipe replaced with the new style pipe, and some early tanks had their six antenna arms replaced with eight arms or removed all together, which was a very common occurrence.

Deployment

The T-35 was first assigned to the 5th Heavy Tank Regiment on 12 December 1935 when the regiment was reorganised into the 5th Independent Heavy Tank Brigade. In 1938, after the summer manoeuvres, the brigade was transferred to the Kiev Special Military District where it was renamed the 14th Heavy Tank Brigade.

Forty-eight of the tanks were later transferred to the 8th Mechanised Corps, two were sent to the Moscow Military District, and six were sent to the 2nd Saratov Tank School. In June 1941, on the eve of Operation Barbarossa, five tanks were going through capital repairs; they were being stripped of old or obsolete parts to be replaced with fresh or modern parts, back in Kharkiv. This is how the stage was set on the eve of what would become known as the Great Patriotic War.

SU-14 Heavy Artillery Platform

The Soviet T-35A tank, like almost every tank in the Red Army, was evaluated for conversion into other types of vehicles. Indeed, the Red Army was far ahead of other nations when it came to standardization of chassis. Classic examples of this include the extensive use of the T-26 light tanks for alternative roles such as prime movers, assault guns, and even anti-aircraft platforms. Naturally, the T-35's chassis would be easy to develop into other useful vehicles. One of the best known of these is a self-propelled gun project—the SU-14.

In 1933, directives from 17 September 1931 demanded a mobile artillery piece utilizing multiple heavy artillery, ranging in calibre from 107 mm to 305 mm. Shortly after, a prototype vehicle that could be fitted with a variety of guns was drawn up on the basis of an altered T-35 chassis. While able to test a variety of guns, the idea was that one gun would be selected for standard production of the vehicle. It took almost two years to create the first prototype as the T-35 chassis chosen was not ready for such large modifications. The basic chassis needed to be heavily altered in order to accommodate the necessary equipment to operate the 203-mm B-3 howitzer that was chosen for this prototype.

However, after the two years, one prototype was ready—the SU-14. The basic T-35 chassis was lengthened to accommodate the fighting compartment, and the bogie arms on the suspension were redesigned. The SU-14's fighting compartment was a rectangular open-topped box, housing a 203-mm B-4 gun, two small cranes for ammunition loading, and rear access door with a ball mount for a DT-29 machine gun.

The driver sat in a small cab next to the engine fan, which was in a new hexagonal box with a grill cover that could be opened for maintenance. This arrangement was in fact the reversal of the T-35, with the tank effectively driving and fighting backwards. The side skirts were very similar to the regular production T-35s, with the exception of small holes in the skirts for access to the suspension.

Almost immediately after the first prototype was completed, the second SU-14 prototype was ordered. This prototype, known as the SU-14-1, was very similar to the previous prototype, with a major exception of the gun; this time, it mounted a smaller calibre 152-mm B-10. The side skirts were redesigned, which were almost identical to late production T-35s, save for missing the last piece over the front idler wheel and one over the drive wheel. In addition, distinctive round access ports were implemented on the skirts.

After extensive testing, both prototypes were handed over to Factory No. 185 (the famous Kirov Plant) in January 1940 to have new armoured cabs fitted over the gun and fighting compartment. However, the upgrade was not complete until March due to the delayed arrival of the armour from the Izhora Plant. These plates were 30–50 mm thick and heavily affected the driving performance of the tanks.

Another less drastic modification was made after trials on 27 March 1940. The road wheels were changed from rubber to steel because rubber wheels were found to degrade too quickly. The SU-14 project was dropped as it was found that the tanks were too long and cumbersome for the desired role. In addition, the new KV tanks that had been designed in late 1939 were already being updated with an artillery piece for direct fire support—the KV-2. Nevertheless, both vehicles joined the T-35-1, T-35-2, and TG tank at Kubinka, which was the Red Army testing facility outside Moscow, sometimes known as 'The Polygon'.

The Great Patriotic War saw these machines deployed in the defence of Kubinka. Along with the prototype T-100Y, these two SU-14 prototypes were deployed in the 'Separate heavy battalion of special purpose'. Unfortunately, no wartime information survives on the combat of these artillery pieces. It is possible they never fired a shot; however, they could have engaged targets from a long range. Both prototypes survived the war, but in 1960, the SU-14 was scrapped. The SU-14-1 is, fortunately, still on display at Kubinka.

The SU-14 prototype before being equipped with an armoured cab—quite clearly a very exposed system. The suspension has been very heavily modified. The square access ports in the hull are evident here. (*Maxim Kolomiets*)

The SU-14-1 prototype. Notice how different the suspension system is with simplified skirts with round access holes. The gun is also a less powerful 152-mm gun. (*Maxim Kolomiets*)

The SU-14-1 prototype from above. The two cranes at the rear are for lifting shells into the tank. The driver's compartment can be seen at the front lift, which in reality is the rear right as this system drives backwards. (*Maxim Kolomiets*)

2

The Battle of Brody and the Battle at Verba

On 22 June 1941, the Soviet Union was attacked by the armed forces of Germany and its allies. Of the forty-eight T-35 tanks deployed in the 8th Mechanised Corps, all were lost by 1 September. A single T-35 still survives to this day: chassis number 0197-7, one of the tanks from the Saratov Tank School. However, the documentation from the 67th and 68th Tank Regiments also survives, which gives us an insight into the combat debut of the T-35 (Tables 2 and 3).

There was only one real documented engagement in which the T-35 tank was used; it was destroyed in combat then later photographed. On 24 June 1941, two days after the invasion of the USSR, the German Army found a gap between the Soviet 5th and 6th Armies. This was exploited to create a corridor lead by the 11th Panzer Division followed by other units, including the 48th Motorised Division and the 16th Panzer Division. The Red Army was not unaware that the German Army (*Panzergruppe* 1) had found this gap, and so moved to meet the Germans on their flanks. The Soviet 8th, 9th, 15th, and 19th Mechanised Corps were ordered to meet the Germans and engage them. Of the forty-eight T-35s that were deployed in the 8th Mechanised Corps, all tanks were lost in the withdrawal from their garrisons east of Lviv to Zhytomyr.

Some T-35s were driven from Dubno to Zhytomyr, having originally been deployed between Lviv and Przemysl; they were chased all the way by the German front line. Most T-35s were lost on this march rather than in combat due to mechanical issues. However, a few tanks turned around and fought back, inflicting some casualties onto the Germans. The bulk of the fighting that involved the T-35 was between Dubno (which was recaptured on 28 June by the 8th Mechanised Corps) and Brody, which was never liberated in the counter attack. It was between these two towns that a handful of T-35s engaged the enemy.

According to the records of the men of the 16th Panzer Division and the records of the losses of the 34th Tank Division, four T-35s, two BT-7s, two T-26s, and a KV-1 attacked the German flank at Verba. This was where elements of the 16th Panzer Division were laid up. This village had previously been captured on 27 June. It is reported that the Soviets succeeded in cutting the communications between the 16th Panzer Division and the 6th Army. However, all of the attacking Soviet tanks were lost in the engagement. It is uncertain but likely that two tanks—148-39 and 220-25—were destroyed by air attack as the death certificates of the crew members describe them being 'killed by Bird'; however, this could refer to the name of a village. Ukranian villages often had place names that were the same as animals—for example in the Lviv Oblast, two separate villages can be found with the name 'Hedgehog'. Nevertheless, the two other T-35s—0200-0 and 988-16—have been photographed with multiple penetrations. The Russians did not have the monopoly on casualties; at least two German Panzer IIIs and a Panzer II were knocked out in this engagement.

T-35 0200-9 was lost in fighting at Sasiv. However, it was not knocked out, but rather abandoned in what can only be described as a traffic jam. T-35 148-25 was also lost due to enemy action with a penetration to the smoke generator that caused the tank to catch fire. There is evidence that other tanks were knocked out in combat, but this is uncertain. There is photographic evidence of tanks 339-30, 0200-5, and 744-61, which suggests combat damage; images also indicate that 339-30 suffered multiple hits to the main turret pedestal. Also, the rear fan covers of all tanks being dislodged due to damage. At least one T-35 (148-30) was abandoned after engaging the Germans in Kharkiv.

Heading from east to west, the following were abandoned on this road: T-35s 220-25 and 148-39 both exploded, possibly by air attack approximately 50 metres apart; two BT-7s, one sporting air identification triangles; T-26 model 1939 with air identification triangles; T-35 0200-0 with multiple hits; and a KV-1 with multiple hits. New evidence suggests that 988-16 was actually lost before the village of Verba. All tanks spread out over approximately 2 miles of road. A T-26 model 1939 was also lost alongside 988-16 There exists two known photographs of this battle.

The only film footage of a T-35A in 'combat' was in the Russian propaganda film *Battle Before Moscow* (*Разгром немецких войск под Москвой*); the Soviet name for this film translates directly as *Moscow Strikes Back*. The featured tank was possibly one of the 148 chassis numbers as it features the single turret hatch and, interestingly, is the only known example with combat lights.

This would normally be the end of the combat story of the T-35A; however, one T-35 was used in combat by the unlikeliest of users. T-35A 715-62 was captured by the Germans in 1941 in Lviv. The tank was selected to be returned to Kummersdorf to undergo testing by the OKH (*Oberkommando des Heeres*). That tank sat there from late 1941 until April 1945. German forces used all available tanks at their disposal to try to stop the Russian advance into Berlin. T-35A 715-62 was removed from stowage and was stripped of guns, tracks, and skirts. It was recaptured by Russian forces on 22 April 1945. One photograph of this tank exists after recapture by Russian forces.

Photographically, there are at most forty-eight individual tanks, not all from the 67th and 68th Tank Regiments. Some crossover may exist within photographs of particularly rare examples. However, this still leaves at least eleven tanks unaccounted for. This book gives a good representation of the rarity of individual photos.

In this publication, the story of the T-35 will be told in photographs. T-35s with chassis numbers discovered and undiscovered have stories to tell through the photographic evidence, as well as in the evidence presented though the production tables. In this publication, only five T-35s still have unknown chassis number tanks, whereas thirty-five have been discovered.

The aftermath of the Battle of Brody. This KV-1 probably served in the 67th Regiment of the 34th Tank Division of the 8th Mechanised Corps. It was lost on the road from Ptyche to Verba along with the four T-35s. Notice a T-35A (chassis number 0200-0) in the far-left corner. It appears that this KV-1 was retreating, possibly after the other tanks were lost. The rear of the turret is peppered with hits, but interestingly, has no penetrations.

An artist's impression of the Battle of Verba. This picture depicts the battle about three-quarters of the way through. T-35 0200-0 is already in the ditch between the main road and the support road. T-35 148-39 has been bombed and has exploded. T-35 220-25 is exploding in a ball of fire; an air attack likely destroyed it. It is unknown when the Panzer IIIs were lost, and this art piece depicts them still fighting. Interestingly and importantly, T-35 988-16 is rolling down the support road, still fighting. This tank would, along with a T-26, make it past this point and would eventually be lost further up the road.

The Battle of Brody and the Battle at Verba

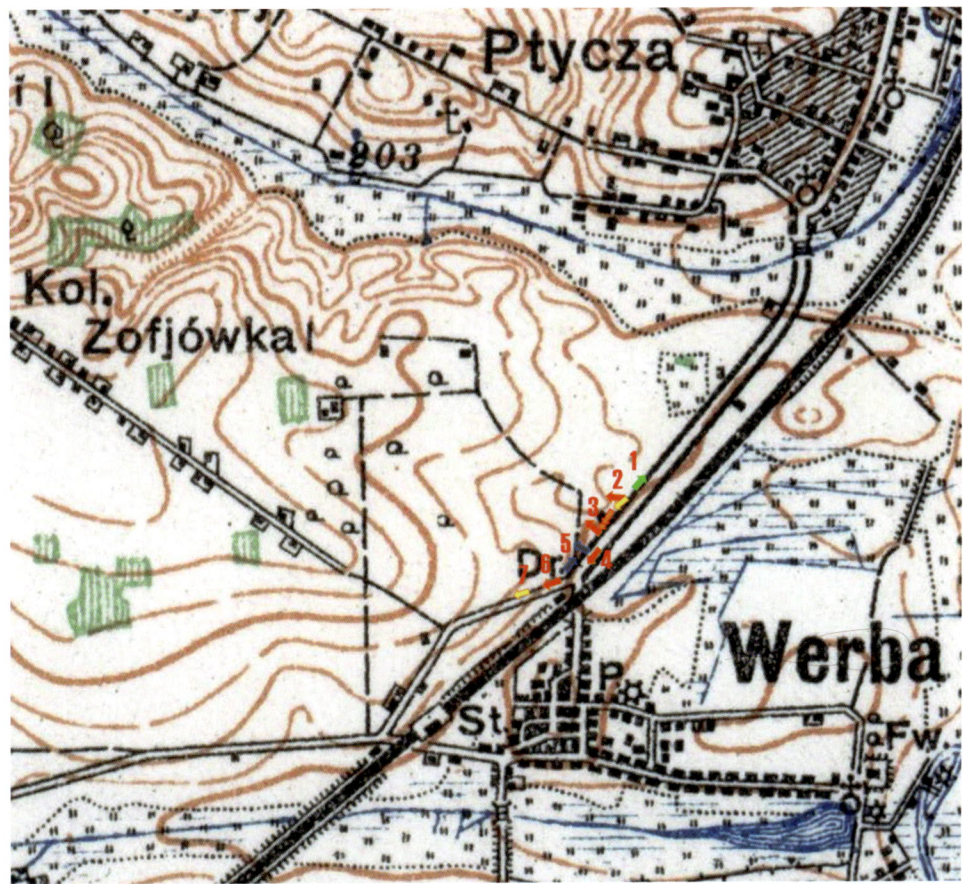

The Battle of Verba was a tremendous disaster for the Russians, losing no fewer than nine tanks and countless men; however, the German forces did lose at least two Panzer IIIs and a collection of trucks and personnel. The map shows the locations of the tanks on that fateful day.

1. The destroyed KV-1 was possibly the last tank to be lost in the battle. Interestingly, the tank faces east, indicating that it was attempting to retreat.
2. T-35A 0200-0 and a T-26 Model 1939. Originally, the T-26 was lost on the road, but was later moved to the same ditch that 0200-0 was lost in.
3. No. 148-39 along with the two BT-7s.
4. No. 220-25. Interestingly, this tank and the previous were completely destroyed by air attack.
5. The two Panzer IIIs Ausf.Gs that were lost in the Verba battle.
6. T-35A 988-16. This tank made it furthest west of all the T-35s lost. Behind the tank on the bend, several German tracks were totally destroyed.
7. The furthest tank west was a sole T-26 Model 1939.

A T-35 crawls across a parade square in Kiev. This tank has a single turret hatch, Amplified MG turrets, and an eight arm antenna.

1934	1935	1936	1937	1938	1939
148-11	339-30	220-25	0197-1	0197-2	744-62*
148-19	339-48	220-27	0197-6	0197-7	744-63*
148-22	339-75	220-28	0217-35	0200-0	744-64*
148-25	339-79	220-29	196-94	0200-4	744-65*
148-30	339-78	220-43	196-95	0200-8	744-66*
148-31	288-11	288-43	196-96	0200-5	744-67*
148-39	288-14	288-65	988-15	0200-9	
148-40	288-41	288-74	988-16	234-34*	
148-41		0183-3	988-17	234-35*	
148-50		0183-5	988-18	234-42*	
		0138-7		744-61*	
		537-70			
		537-80			
		537-90			
		715-61			
		7115-62			

Table 1: Table of the chassis numbers of T-35s and the year of production. Tanks with * are vehicles with a conical turret (some tanks had alternate chassis numbers; these were left out for ease of use).

Fifty-nine tanks are listed in Table 1. There is some contention that two tanks were produced in 1933. However, there is no evidence of this; it is thought that these were two prototypes.

67th Tank Regiment	
0197-1	25 June, burned main clutch 20 km east of Gorodok.
288-43	26 June, crashed, the main friction clutch is provided in disrepair, arms lifted in the district of the town (Gorodok).
744-62	26 June, burnt out disc friction clutches in Gorodok.
183-7	29 June, gearbox failure near Lviv.
234-35	30 June, capsized in a river up the tracks in an area with Ivashkovtsy and made unusable.
288-65	30 June, gearbox failure between Krasne and Busk.
537-70	30 June, damaged left brake pad, abandoned by crew before recovery between Olesno and Ozhydiv.
744-67	2 July, bursting of the crankshaft; left in Zhadin.
234-42	3 July, tank crashed, burst cylinder and burned the main clutch. Made unusable. Armament removed in Zapytiv.
0200-5	8 July, crashed and burned brake band, made unusable, arms lifted in the district of Zolochiv.
744-66	9 July, burned the main and steering clutches in the district with. Byaozheno; made unusable, arms lifted.
744-65	9 July, failure of the gearbox. Left between Ternopil and Volochysk.
0197-6	9 July, clutch failure and dead batteries near Dzerdzuno.
183-6	9 July, brake failure near Volochysk.
744-64	Abandoned with Nos 196-95 and 330-75 in need of capital repair in Gorodok, arms lifted.
196-95	Abandoned with Nos 744-64 and 330-75 in need of capital repair in Gorodok, arms lifted.
339-75	Abandoned with Nos 744-64 and 196-95 in need of capital repair in Gorodok, arms lifted.

Table 2: The losses of the 67th Tank Regiment are unfavourable to say the least, with all of its vehicles succumbing to mechanical failure. However, this table is not entirely accurate, with many dates being incorrect.

68th Tank Regiment	
220-29	Stuck in bog at Sudova Vyshnia. Weapons and optics removed. The vehicle was left behind during withdrawal.
217-35	Stuck in bog at Sudova Vyshnia. Weapons and optics removed. The vehicle was left behind during withdrawal.
715-61	24 June, gearbox and fan drive failure. Abandoned 29 June 15 km past Lviv. Cannon breeches, optics, and ammo removed and buried.
0200-4	24 June, left in non-operational state in Sudova Vyshnia. Weapons and optics removed from vehicles. On the orders of Major Shorik, regiment deputy commander, the vehicles were blown up during unit's withdrawal.
196-94	24 June, left in non-operational state in Sudova Vyshnia. Weapons and optics removed from vehicles. On the orders of Major Shorik, regiment deputy commander, the vehicles were blown up during unit's withdrawal.
148-50	24 June, left in non-operational state in Sudova Vyshnia. Weapons and optics removed from vehicles. On the orders of Major Shorik, regiment deputy commander, the vehicles were blown up during unit's withdrawal.
537-80	24 June, crashed (broken transmission and gearboxes) in the area of Gorodok, the machine was left in place.

0200-8	26 June, broke crankshaft in Sudova Vyshnia area on 23 June. Left behind by crew. Weapons and optics removed.
220-27	24 June, crashed (broken transmission and gearboxes) in the area of Gorodok, the machine left in place.
288-14	28 June, disappeared without a trace along with crew near Zapytiv village on 29 June.
148-25	29 June, final drive malfunction. Left by crew in Zapytiv village. Optics and weapons removed and buried by crew.
183-16	29 June, gearbox failure. Left 20 km from Lviv.
288-11	29 June, fell off bridge, burned down along with crew near Lviv.
715-62	29 June, fan drive failure, connections burned in motor. Cannon firing mechanisms buried, MGs removed. Tank abandoned by crew in Lviv.
988-17	29 June, needing capital repairs near Lviv.
988-16	30 June, knocked out and burned down in combat in Ptyche village.
339-48	30 June, knocked out during withdrawal in Kamianka area and burned down.
0200-0	30 June, knocked out and burned between Verba and Ptyche.
220-25	30 June, Knocked out in combat near Ptyche, burned down.
183-3	30 June, engine breakdown, left by crew in Kamianka, weapons and ammo buried.
148-39	30 June, knocked out by enemy near Verba and burned down.
744-61	30 June, suffered breakdowns (transmissions and final drives). Left behind during withdrawal.
339-30	30 June, knocked out by enemy and burned down. Weapons and optics removed from all three vehicles (339-30, 744-61, and 0200-9) and buried.
0200-9	30 June, suffered breakdowns (transmissions and final drives). Left behind during withdrawal.
339-68	30 June, accident with on board clutch. Shells hit and burned at Brody.
744-63	1 July, piston issue. Abandoned on the way from Zlochiv to Ternopil. Firing mechanism and MGs removed and handed to the division's transport vehicles on 2 July.
988-15	1 July, gearbox breakdown, gears 1-X and reverse broken. Left in Zlochiv. Weapons, optics, ammo removed and handed over to Zlochiv military unit warehouse.
148-22	1 July, gearbox failure in Sasiv.
148-2?	Unknown date in July, gearbox breakdown. Left in forest near Sasiv village. Optics and firing mechanisms of cannons buried.
288-74	1 July, main clutch and final drive breakage. Set on fire by crew on 2 July near Ternopil.
196-96	2 July, final drive breakdown. Left by crew near Ternopil. Weapons were not removed.
234-34	4 July, main clutch burned, stuck while fording river near Ternopil. Abandoned by crew. MGs removed and handed to transport vehicles.

Table 3: The 68th Tank Regiments losses are more accurate than those of the 67th Tank regiments, especially with dates; however, inaccuracies occur with locations.

While tanks are missing and information about locations is generally poor, it is interesting to review these tables to see how poorly the tanks performed in combat. Of the tanks missing from this table, we know that two tanks were deployed in the defence of Moscow; none survived. Tank 197-7 still exists due to being a part of the Saratov Tank School. The tank is an excellent example of a mid-production tank, with the late exhaust and P-40 AA Mount. This tank is located at the Kubinka Tank Museum outside Moscow.

3

The Combat Debut of the T-35A Tank in Photos

The following is a breakdown of T-35s in chassis number order. Unknown chassis numbers are situated between the tank issued with a single turret hatch and tanks upgraded to P-40 AA mount standard.

T-35A 148-30

T-35A 148-30 was built in 1934; it was the fifth T-35 ever built (excluding prototype tanks). It appears that 148-30 was at the KhPZ when the war broke out, and therefore was not in Lviv with its brothers during the destruction of the 34th Tank Division. Photographs show that the tank had several major upgrades during its career, including replacement of the six-arm antenna with an eight-arm antenna. However, it retained the original exhaust pipe and driver's vision hatch. The exhaust was a far more uncommon feature.

This tank was not part of 67th or 68th Tank Regiments and was most likely delivered directly to the tank school in Kharkiv. After German forces approached the city, it was then handed over to the defenders of Kharkiv. Evidence suggests that the tank belonged to the Separate Armoured (anti-tank) Unit. This unit consisted of twenty-five T-27s, thirteen KhTZ-16s, five T-26s, and four T-35s. Hereafter, the tank was lost, as shown by the photographs, and is only mentioned in the Wehrmacht's 57th Infantry Division's combat report of the capture of Kharkiv. The 57th engaged 'four light and two heavy tanks' on 22 October 1941. Five of them, according to the report, were hit; one retreated 'strongly heeling' (it was damaged).

Another report by the department of 'The Search and Collection of Trophies' within the headquarters of the 55th Army Corps (Wehrmacht) states: 'In Grigorovka [south-western part of Kharkiv] found intact one Russian tank. Armament: three guns, one 7.62 cm, two 4.5 cm, and five machine guns.'

The location of this tank would have been Barkalova Street, about 40 miles west of the Kharkiv Professional College, just opposite Building 14. As the tank was left, it slowly began to degrade, with more and more parts being removed over time. The Germans, even though the war was still being fought, used a lot of resources to dismantle tanks. During the winter of 1941, the Germans added a number on the side of the tank—'15045/B'—which is thought to be a 'captured' tank serial number. The last photographs show the tank without skirts, track, and sub turrets.

No. 148-30 shortly after it was lost. Interestingly, there does not appear to be any damage to the tank. It has as early exhaust pipe. A close inspection of the turret shows how the six-arm antenna was upgraded to an eight-arm antenna with the original foot plate left on the turret behind the support stip.

No. 148-30, *c.* late October 1941. While blurry, it is easy to make out some technical features, such as the early exhaust and the unamplified MG turret faces.

No. 148-30 after the snow started to fall. Noticeable features are the deployed ladder on the skirts and the German additions to the tank. The red star on the hull has been highlighted with a white outline and the turret cheek has a serial number written onto it. (*John Prigent*)

Above: From the same collection as the previous photograph, 148-30 sits under its snowy blanket, now nothing more than a good photo opportunity for German soldiers. The serial number on the cheek is 15045/B. Shortly after the spring of 1942, the MG turrets were removed from the tank, swiftly followed by the skirts, track, and peripherals. (*John Prigent*)

Below: T-35 148-30 sat in her position for much of 1942; however, she was slowly stripped of turrets and skirts. In this picture, the two 45-mm gun turrets are missing. The turret's paint had warn away over the winter, revealing the pre-war colour bands on the turret.

T-35A 148-39

T-35A 148-39 was manufactured in 1934 and was the seventh T-35 produced. This tank was upgraded more drastically than her sister, 148-30. The biggest changes were the late exhaust pipe with two exterior pipes featuring the internal muffler. In addition, the six-armed antenna was completely removed, leaving only the square foot plates.

No. 148-39 was deployed with the 68th Tank Regiment, and was lost spectacularly in a huge explosion on 30 June 1941. That day, four T-35s attacked the 16th Panzer Division at Verba. This was an action that made-up part of the 8th Mechanised Corps' attempt to encircle the spearhead of Army Group South.

Approaching from Pichya, the four T-35s, along with two BT-7s, a KV-1, and a T-26 rolled down the highway. The highway in question was a two-land road, and it would appear that at least one T-35—148-39—was in the right-hand lane, whereas 0200-0 was in the left lane; it is likely that 220-25 was also in the left lane. A single combat photograph of the engagement exists that clearly illustrates the battles conclusion.

The photographs of the battle show 0200-0 already in the ditch between the two roads, as well as 220-25, already on fire and without a turret. Interestingly, 148-39 appears to already have been destroyed, but is just out of view in most images. One BT-7 is visible where it remained after the battle ended, and another is driving towards its final resting position (434). The last T-35, 988-16, is often seen still intact, driving past the wreck of 148-39; new evidence suggests the tank was lost on the other side of Verba.

The death certificates of the crews of 148-39 and 220-25 suggest that the tanks were destroyed by air attack; this seems likely, seeing as what was left of 148-39 was a burned wreck. All the turrets were dislodged and most blown far from the tank. Debris from the battle in the following photographs is very telling of the destructive course of events. One photograph in particular clearly shows two Panzer IIIs knocked out in the road by 220-25.

An interesting point with the damage of 148-39 was the main turret. The main turret on a T-35 was connected to a rotating turret floor by five arms. On three arms were seats for the crew; the centre seat was a folding seat for the main hatch, while the other two were used for stowage of ammunition. When the turret blew off the tank, the turret floor seems have stayed in the tank, but was totally obliterated. Despite sounding fairly unique, this is a situation that actually occurred a few times with mixed results. Some tanks retained the turret floor in the pedestal, while others were presumably dislodged with the turret.

T-35A 148-50

The last T-35 of the 148 series was 148-50. It was manufactured in 1934 and was the tenth T-35 produced. Unfortunately, due to the state of disrepair in photographs, some technical features are obscured. However, some features remain visible, such as the main antenna. Like 148-30, it has been updated from six arms to eight arms. However, the upgrade was done differently to 148-30. The front foot plate on the left is overlarge, and the original foot plates for the middle and rear plate are still in place, unlike 148-30, which only has it on the middle arm.

The aftermath of the Battle of Verba left many Soviet vehicles rendered disabled. T-35A 148-39 is no exception as seen with no superstructure left and turrets scattered around. Two BT-7s are also left—one is charred with the other apparently damaged less.

No. 220-25 is on Verba road, with two destroyed Panzer IIIs to the right of it. Debris is scattered up the road; these include a Russian lorry cab and a Panzer II turret that most likely was lost two days before the battle.

The wreck of 148-39 from the left side. From this angle, the placing of the turret is clear. Close inspection on the turret indicates the remnants of the six antenna arms. T-35A 0200-0 can be seen in the background alongside the T-26 in the ditch.

The interior of 148-39. Starting from the top left, there is the hole that is usually capped, which gives access to the fuel tank. To the right of this is the rear 45-mm gun. As is evident, the turret has been blown off and most likely landed on the tank's back. The access hatch at the rear of the 45-mm gun was used for removal of the gun itself. The dividing wall between the 45-mm gun compartment and the engine compartment is evident. There is a machine gun ammunition rack laying on the engine side of the wall. On the left side of the photo, this would have been again divided by a wall. This wall has sustained the greatest damage. Originally, the pedestal wall would have been covered in ammunition racks for 76.2-mm gun ammunition and DT machine gun magazines.

No. 148-39 in July 1941. The damage to the suspension gives a strange profile.

Above: On the turret, only six antenna feet can be seen. This tank was not updated to the standard eight arms.

Below: No. 148-50 shortly after the tank was abandoned. The wooden A-frame has been used to lift the engine out of the tank. A 45-mm shell sits on top of the rear MG turret. The front foot plate is clearly visible too. Take note of some of the debris, including DT-29 ammunition and magazines, plus the jack for changing the tension of the track is on the ground. A second T-35 can also be seen behind the tank; this is 196-94.

After the tank had sat in a field for a short amount of time, 148-50 was used by the Germans as a tank for infantry training. The large plate is next to the support strip. The white 'x' and 'o' markings on the tank denote 37-mm or 20-mm gun hits. Interestingly, the rear fender has been placed on the forward fender of the tank.

The aftermath of infantry training on 148-50. The white crosses mark the hits on the tank from AT rounds. From this angle, the rear antenna feet for the original antenna is visible. Also note the graffiti on both tanks' red stars. (*Sergey Lotarev*)

T-35A 148-50 was deployed with the 68th Tank Regiment; when war broke, it was being repaired in the village of Sudova Vyshnia, which was being used as the repair centre of the 68th Tank Regiment. Within the village, four T-35s were lost, all from the 68th. Three tanks—148-50, 196-94, and 0200-4—were at the repair centre undergoing capital repairs. One other tank, 715-61, was lost while travelling though the village.

After capture by the Wehrmacht, the tanks sat in their positions for a month or so before they were used for anti-tank training. It was initially shot at with anti-tank weapons, and photographs of the tank with white crosses on it from hits depict this. In addition, the tanks were attacked with flame throwers and grenades; 196-94 was destroyed.

Unidentified 148-XX

This is an interesting example of how the documentation of the losses can be a hindrance as well as a helpful tool for identification. This tank is listed as being lost due to gearbox failure and left in a forest near Sasiv; however, the last two numbers of the chassis number are missing in the original table of losses and information in the table regarding this tank is incorrect.

The chassis number as written in the losses of the 68th Tank Regiment as '148-2' with a number almost totally missing because the document has degraded over time. However, it could be a three or a five. The issue is that both chassis numbers that are 148 with the second half beginning with two have been accounted for. No. 148-22 was lost in a field just outside of Sasiv, having been destroyed by enemy action, whereas 148-25 was knocked out due to enemy action in the village of Zapytiv. The documentation for the losses of the 68th Tank Regiment describe 148-XX's fate as: '148-2X gearbox breakdown. Left in forest near Sasiv village [unknown date, but listed as July by "7"]. Optics and firing mechanisms of cannons buried.'

The chassis numbers that this machine could be are: 148-11, 148-19, 148-31, 148-40, and 148-41. It is thought that at two of these chassis numbers can be attributed to the T-35 at the Saratov Tank School and the T-35 deployed in Moscow in December 1941.

However, the story of this machine is deeper than previously described in the table of losses. One photograph so far exists of this tank; it depicts a T-35 in a small wooded area. However, the picture also deepens the mystery. Technical features include unamplified MG turrets, the early driver's access hatch, and the early exhaust. Although these are all typical of a 148 chassis number, the main turret throws a spanner into the works.

The turret initially looks like a normal T-35A 148 turret (namely, a single turret hatch and foot-plates for the antenna that indicate changes to the antenna from a six-arm to an eight-arm antenna). However, the tank also has a second support strip on the turret. This is highly unusual for a 148 chassis number as this strip was not introduced until 1936, whereas 148 chassis numbers were introduced in 1934.

The leading theory by experts, which there is some evidence for, is that some T-35s were returned to the factory to have their turret either replaced or repaired due to cracking. This is a good explanation of the second strip of support not only being there in the first place, but also because it is too far rearward for a standard production second strip of support on the turret.

This incredibly rare machine is only known for sure from this photograph. While it might be referred to in the table of losses, this is not certain. Visible over the large foot plate is the clothes line antenna, a clear indication that this is indeed a 148 chassis number. The turret, strangely enough, has two turret support strips. This is likely due to the tank being returned to the factory for repair in the pre-war period and to be updated to a new standard.

Whatever the actual answer, this machine is highly unusual and a very rare machine indeed. Only one photograph has surfaced of this machine rather recently. To further complicate issues, there is combat damage evident on the smoke generator and some damage on the turret. This was likely from German tank shooting at the tank 'just in case' the tank was still active and just 'playing dead'.

T-35A 339-30

This was the first T-35 produced in 1935 and the first of the new chassis numbers. The only outward difference between the 339s and 148s was the addition of the new eight-armed antenna. Sometime in the late 1930s, the tank was also given amplified MG turret faces. T-35A 339-30 was the eleventh T-35 produced. This tank was later upgraded by the addition of the late driver's vision hatch and the removal of the clothes-line antenna.

On 22 June 1941, this tank was deployed with the 68th Tank Regiment. Unfortunately, the location of the tank when it was lost is unknown. Fortunately, some details are not.

No. 339-30 very shortly after the tank was lost. The '=' divisional markings denote the 68th Tank Regiment. Also, the gear system for the rear fan is on the engine deck. The position of the wood saw indicates that the tank has the late stowage. The placing of the tools on the fender of the tank was modified as production continued, and it is another marker to look out for on these tanks, with early stowage having the wood saw next to the radiator intake, whereas the late stowage has the wood saw next to the rear MG turret.

No. 339-30 on 2 December 1942. The tank has deteriorated substantially. Notice the late driver's vision hatch. Just visible is the rear access hatch on the 45-mm gun turrets, which were used for maintenance and removal of the gun. Also see that the MG turrets have been removed. This appears to be common with T-35s being deconstructed by Germans and was a part of their dismantling process.

On 30 June, 339-30, 0200-9, and 744-61 appear to have been travelling as a group on the edge of a wooded area when they were knocked out. All the tanks have clear evidence of combat damage. The most obvious damage to the tank is the displaced rear fan. In addition, photographic evidence exists of multiple hits to the turret pedestal.

The tank was lost around the same location, possibly in front of 339-30, displaying very similar damage. No. 744-61 is one of the rarest T-35s to find on film; outwardly identical to 744-62, it was lost directly in front and about 20 m to the left of 339-30. Only two known photographs have this tank in shot.

T-35A 339-75

No. 339-75 is a fairly standard and early production T-35. It was made in 1935 and was the thirteenth T-35 manufactured. The only visible upgrades are the late driver's vision hatch and presumably the late exhaust. In addition, this tank had amplified machine gun turret faces. These were 10-mm plates that were attached to the face of the MG turrets, which helped protect the gun and the crewman.

It was deployed with the 67th Tank Regiment when the war broke out, and was stationed at a repair centre in the village of Gorodok. Both Gorodok and Sudova Vyshnia (again, which was the repair centre of the 68th Tank Regiment) were about 30 miles to the east of Lviv. Both villages were captured on the second day of Operation Barbarossa (24 June). Along with six other T-35s, 339-75 was lost in Gorodok on that day. Two other tanks—196-95 and 744-64—were also deployed with the 67th Tank Regiment and located in the repair yard; the latter was a last production conical tank, identical to 744-67.

Along with these three tanks, two identical T-35s from the 68th Tank Regiment were lost in the same field as these three tanks—220-27 and 537-80. Both tanks have not been identified due to how similar they look. Out of the repair centre to the north of the main road (now the T1465 highway), two more T-35s were lost. One tank was a conical-turreted tank (744-62) and the other was an unidentified P-40 AA machine gun mount tank.

No. 339-75 sat in this field with the other tanks and like the tanks at Sudova Vyshnia, they were used as infantry and anti-tank training, albeit to a much lesser extent. Film footage even exists of the tanks being shot at by a Pak 38 50-mm gun. No. 339-75 is also famous for being adorned with a list of specifications by German soldiers.

T-35A 228-14

T-35A 228-14 was manufactured in 1935 and was the sixteenth T-35 produced. As was common, the tank was updated with later features, which included the late exhaust and amplified MG turret faces. Deployed with the 68th tank Regiment, it was lost on 28 June. Interestingly, the tank does not feature the '=' divisional markings or a red star on the skirt; this is highly unusual for T-35s.

No. 339-75 sits at the Gorodok repair centre. The track is piled up on the floor in front of the vehicle. (*Sergey Lotarev*)

No. 339-75 sitting in the field at Gorodok. Notice the amplified MG turret faces and the late driver's vision hatch.

No. 228-14 shortly after it was lost. The rear 45-mm gun turret periscope still has the protective cap equipped. The tank has late exhaust and two exposed transmission hatches at the rear of the tank. The motorcycle is part of the 125th Infantry Division's Reconnaissance Battalion.

This photo of 228-14 could be earlier than the previous image due to the position of the tank on the road. The transmission hatches are on the floor and the amplification is on the MG turret face.

No. 288-14 unceremoniously dumped at the side of the road. The tracks have been removed and white warnings have been painted onto the fender. Also take note of 'property of the OKH' on the turret and smoke generator. The OKH was the *Oberkommando des Heeres* (German High Command).

Above and below: No. 228-14 in May 1942. This tank had the late driver's vision hatch and the open headlights. Interestingly, 'property of OKH' has been crossed out on the right side of the turret.

The tank was lost in the village of Velyki Pidlisky to the west of Lviv. According to the combat report, it was simply 'missing in action'. It is unclear what caused this tank to be lost; however, the records also tell a tale about mechanical failure, especially with the transition. This was a huge issue with the tank—a tank this long often had issues with the track and engines as the length caused by the tank to twist.

Initially left on the right side of the road, the tank was moved to the right curb between bollards that line the road. The track was removed and 'property of the OKH' was written all over the tank.

T-35 220-25

T-35 220-25 was the first T-35 produced in 1936 and the eighteenth vehicle produced overall. It was the first to feature the second strip of supporting armour on the turret side. This was situated behind the third foot plate of the eight-armed antennae. The reason for the implementation of this was due to the redesigning of the composite parts of the turret. Rather than being manufactured from four plates, the turret was now made from six plates.

The tank was upgraded quite heavily during its service career, although some specific features remain unknown due to the severity of the combat damage on the tank. However, it is known that the tank was equipped with the late exhaust, and the late driver's vision hatch, but most interestingly the tank was equipped with the late solid front idler wheel and the 'BT' style driver's access hatch. This is an uncommon upgrade and was a feature of the last four tanks manufactured. These features indicate that the tank was returned to the factory for repairs between 1939 and 1941.

This picture clearly demonstrates the severe damage inflicted on 220-25. Noteworthy technical features include the internal dividing wall visible in the rear section of the tank. (*Sergey Lotarev*)

No. 220-25 was equipped in the 68th Tank Regiment and was involved in heavy fighting on 30 June, when elements of the 68th Tank Regiment engaged the Wehrmacht on the infamous Verba road. As evidenced by the photographs, 220-25 was doomed to suffer a massive internal explosion that seems to have completely destroyed the main turret, blown off the two DT sub-turrets, and completely dislodged the front 45-mm gun turret. According to the death certificates of the crew, this tank was reportedly destroyed by an aerial attack. The tank sat in the road for a substantial amount of time after this, the hull having effectively been cut in half by the explosion. Eventually, it was moved to the side of the road in those two parts. The damage was so severe that no main turret is evident; therefore, only assumptions can be made that the tank was equipped with '=' divisional markings and possibly no clothes-line antenna as no debris of an antenna has been found.

T-35A 220-28

T-35A 220-28 was produced in early 1936 and was the twentieth T-35 produced. Surprisingly, this T-35 appears to have never gone through any upgrades, retaining all of the factory original features, including the early exterior exhaust and driver's vision hatch; it even has no amplification on the MG turrets. The only feature that changed was the antenna, which was removed, with just the foot plates left.

This tank was in Kharkiv undergoing capital repair when the war broke out, and as the Wehrmacht forces approached the city, it was handed over to the Separate Armoured (anti-tank) Unit. This unit consisted of twenty-five T-27s, thirteen TZ-16s, five T-26s, and four T-35s (148-30, 220-28, 537-90, and 0197-2).

It would appear that this tank was lost towards the end of the Battle of Kharkov as it was left destroyed by its crew on Stalin Prospekt, which was one of the main roads leaving the city. It would also seem that the tank was scuttled and destroyed by its crew on purpose to prevent the tank from falling into German hands. The tank would sit in the road until perhaps as early as October 1941 or as late as May 1942 before being moved onto a grassy area next to the road. The initial damage of the tank removed the two machine gun turrets and dislodged the rear 45-mm gun turret and the main turret. While sitting on the grassy patch, the tank was slowly dismantled. Skirts were removed from the tank, along with the 45-mm gun turrets. The tank was also repeatedly graphited with names and even directions.

As Kharkiv fell from Soviet to German control, the tank changed hands no less than four times. In this exchange, the tank suffered a hit from an anti-tank gun or tank. This was likely from the Germans as the tank was facing east and the hit was on the rear. The position of the tank meant that as the soviets attacked from the east, they would have seen the tank from the front, whereas the German defenders would have seen the rear of the tank.

An interesting point is that the turret was attached to a rotating turret floor by five supports. Thus, when the turret was blown off the tank, the turret ring with the floor plate stayed in place, but the turret walls lifted from the tank. The turret roof was

No. 220-28 shortly after the tank was lost. The MG turret is on the ground next to the tank, as well as the dislodged main turret. The tank has been painted with directions, which was a common feature with knocked-out tanks. The smoke generator has had the side blown off. Originally, a bottle of compressed gas would have been inside the box. The photograph has the name Johannes J. Muller; it is unknown if he was the photographer or a person in the frame.

No. 220-28 after a short time sitting on the street. This is a much more uncommon angle to see the tank as German soldiers marching past the tank often took pictures from the road and from the rear.

The Combat Debut of the T-35A Tank in Photos

Right: There is rarely no better source for tank interiors than photos of their wrecks, and 220-28 is no exception. Take note of the opened engine hatch—the M-17L engine is clearly visible. This was the same engine that powered most of the pre-war Russian medium and heavy tanks. BT-5s and BT-7s were also equipped with this engine. In the rear 45-mm gun turret, all the equipment needed for crewing the gun is visible. The two curved pieces of metal on the turret ring inside the 45-mm gun turret are the back rests for the gunner and loader. With all this equipment inside the tank, room was a huge issue inside the T-35. When fully crewed, there was hardly any room inside to work it, making the tank rather claustrophobic.

Below: No. 220-28, *c.* May 1942. The tank had been moved to the side of the road and parts of the tank have been stripped including the MG turrets and 45-mm gun turrets. Notice the early exhaust, the exposed suspension arms, and the exposed gun replicator. In this photo, the second strip of support on the turret just behind the third antenna arm is just visible. Finally, the rear fan cover has a name graphited onto the rear.

Left and below: No. 220-28, *c.* early 1943. These are some of the last photos of 220-28 and of T-35s in general as German forces soon lost possession of Kharkiv, and Soviet soldiers did not take photographs (with the exceptions of officers). Take note of the exhaust pipe side, normally obscured. Much of the tank has been stripped, including many panels on the tank and the side skirt panels. Evidently, the road wheels are missing on the rearmost bogie. Also, the paint on the main turret has pre-war divisional markings. Even this late, the Germans are using the tank for road markings, with 'XXTI' on the engine access hatch. Someone has written something above the turret cheek; however, all that is discernible is 'ausg'.

One of the last but most interesting photos of 220-28. This photo is taken after the previous two photos, yet the tank had actually sustained further combat damage. This photo was most likely taken just before the Battle of Kursk. Evident is the penetration at the rear of the tank. A shell has hit between the two transmission access hatches, and subsequently removed the bracket on the left, which holds on the transmission hatch itself. The fan cover also has sustained damage, revealing the fan underneath the armour. This has been lifted on the left side.

removed in this explosion. It is unknown what happened to this tank after the war, but it is most likely that it, along with many others, was scrapped by the USSR.

T-35A 288-65

T-35A chassis number 288-65 is one of the more recently identified tanks; however, it should be noted that this tank and 288-14 could be each other's chassis number. This tank was the twenty-fourth tank produced and, while it has the chassis number 288, it was manufactured in 1936, a year after the other earlier 288 chassis. This tank's features include a single turret hatch, one strip of support armour, the late exhaust, and the eight-arm antenna.

This tank was abandoned in the village of Banyunyn, which is on the E40 highway in Lviv Oblast. Unfortunately, a large proportion of T-35s were lost on 30 June, in roughly the same location. Therefore, it is very difficult to confirm the chassis number of this particular vehicle.

In the table of losses, this tank is located as 'near Busk', which is the next village along from Banyunyn. This is closer than 288-14 to Busk, therefore it is more likely this tank is 288-65.

Above: This photo probably dates from mid-1941. It is evident that the rear fan cover is missing. Note the interior exhaust with the two pipes exiting the chassis. For a change, the German soldiers are moving past the tank, and Ukrainian civilians are on the tank inspecting it. For many years, Ukraine was under the oppression of the USSR, and many Ukrainians were very welcoming of German troops. It was common for Ukrainian civilians to be happy to help the German soldiers if it meant the very slim chance of freedom. Unfortunately for them, this would prove not to be the case, with Nazi ideology viewing the Slavic race as 'inferior'.

Below: The tank is seen here in either early or late 1942. The 76.2-mm gun has been removed as has the antenna. The rear fender is missing.

The Combat Debut of the T-35A Tank in Photos 47

There is a new contender for the 'most people on one tank' award. There are no fewer than twenty-nine people on this tank, some of whom are holding artefacts from the tank. This photo could be from as late as autumn 1942. The soldier on the left of the tank on the fender is holding a 76.2-mm KT-28 shell. The soldier on the top row, third from left, is holding a 45-mm gun shell.

No. 183-3 only a short time after it was abandoned. Notice the '=' divisional marking on the turret. Interestingly, the rear fan has the air intake slats closed. An interesting fact is that these were adjustable. In the background is a German truck and the Pak 36 AT gun.

Judging by the shadow on the ground and the position of the tank, this photograph was taken on the same day as the previous one, but in the very early morning; the tank is facing north and is casting a rather large shadow. There are the same German trucks in the rear right of frame and the exact same position of the tow rope. (*Sergey Lotarev*)

Front view of 183-3. This tank had the late driver's vision hatch and the early driver's access hatch. Note the late stowage now visible thanks to the open saw position. It is likely that this is an early photo of 183-3 as the tank has some tree branches resting on it. This was a very common feature with several examples surfacing, including one of 234-42 and an unidentified single-turreted T-35. This was done in a vain attempt to camouflage and hide the tank. (*John Prigent*)

T-35A 183-3

A typical 1936 production T-35, 183-3 was the twenty-fifth T-35 produced. Even this late into the production run, the tanks were still being manufactured with the single turret hatch. This tank was upgraded with the late driver's vision hatch, amplified MG turret faces, and the late exhaust. Like so many others, it also had the antenna removed, leaving just the feet.

This tank was deployed with the 68th Tank Regiment, and remarkably was not lost until 30 June. It was abandoned due to an engine failure, and was left in the village of Bilyi Kamin, (Белый Камень, literally 'White Stone') in the Zolochiv district of Lviv region. The ammunition and optics were removed and buried. This was to stop the Germans from using them.

This tank was located near a Catholic Church with a distinctive dome, which is on the road to Buzhok. This church still exists today. Travelling east along the road, there is a triangular junction on the right. The tank was located about 50 metres down this road, facing north.

T-35A 537-70

T-35A 537-70 was produced in 1936 and was the twenty-seventh T-35 produced. However, it was the third to last single-hatched T-35 made. This tank had the standard upgrades issued to T-35s, including the late exhaust, amplified MG turret faces, the late driver's vision hatch, and the complete removal of the eight-armed antenna; this left only the foot plates intact. The most interesting features, however, are the solid front idler wheel and the 'BT' type driver's access hatch.

The tank was issued to the 67th Tank Regiment, and in the early stages of Operation Barbarossa, the tank was issued with white air identification triangles. These triangles are fairly common on Russian tanks; however, with such a large canvas to play with, the artistic prowess of Russian tank crews came out.

No. 537-70 has two triangles on the left side of the turret between the gun and the pistol port, the second between the two support strips. There was only one triangle on the right side, this was at the very right of the turret between the rear machine gun position and the support strip. There was one triangle on the rear 45-mm gun left cheek. This was on the inside cheek, so unusually out of view. The last visible triangle was on the right-hand smoke generator, behind the jack bracket. This is the object attached to the smoke generator.

Unfortunately, the tank never saw combat as on 30 June, the tank broke down due to brake failure. No. 537-70 was abandoned between the villages of Ozhydiv and Yosypivka, heading east. The current location of the tank would have been on the E40/M06 highway, traveling east from Ozhydiv, just after a five-way junction. The road layout has drastically changed, but the basic direction is the same.

No. 537-70 shortly after the tank was lost. Note the clearly open 'BT' style driver's access hatch, the solid idler wheel, and the white air identification triangles—two are on the left side of the turret, one is at the rear on the right side, one is on the inside cheek of the rear 45-mm gun, and one is on the right-hand side smoke generator (just visible in this image).

No. 537-70 from the same collection as the previous image. The 'BT' style hatch is more obvious here; similarly, the second white triangle is also more clearly visible.

The Combat Debut of the T-35A Tank in Photos

No. 537-70 a short time after the tank was lost. The white air identification triangle can be seen on the rear right side of the tank. The bicycle gives a stark perspective on the size of the tank.

With the damage, features are evident, including the large metal canister in the smoke generator box. This bottle contained a gas that, when mixed with another gas, created smoke. The tank also had the main turret and MG turret laying by the right side; these have been moved.

The tank at a similar date to the previous photograph. There is a soldier in the rear turret.

No. 537-90 during the winter of 1941. Some debris is missing.

T-35A 537-90

T-35A 537-90 was the twenty-ninth and last single-hatched T-35 produced. Unfortunately, due to the damage sustained, some technical features can only be inferred from non-photographic evidence. The tank was upgraded with the late exhaust and the late driver's vision hatch. However, it is unknown whether the tank had a clothes line antenna or not. The turret would have had two support strips.

As with 148-30 and 220-28, 537-90 was situated in Kharkiv when the war broke out. The tank was then deployed with the Separate Armoured (anti-tank) Unit. Again, for reference, this unit consisted of twenty-five T-27s, thirteen KhTZ-16s, five T-26s, and four T-35s, including 148-30, 220-28, 537-90, and 0197-2. Unfortunately, no evidence has been found of 0197-2.

The tank was similar to 220-28 and destroyed by its crew in order to stop the tank falling into the hands of the Germans. The tank was scuttled, completely, removing the main turret from the hull. The tank sat at Voroshilov Street (now Yakir Street); the building behind it still exists.

With the damage, features are evident including the large metal canister in the smoke generator box. This bottle contained a gas that, when mixed with another gas, created smoke. The tank also had the main turret and machine gun turret laying by the right side; these have been moved.

Unknown T-35A (537-80/220-27)

For the T-35 enthusiast, this is a frustrating mystery. There are two T-35s that could be one of two chassis numbers: 537-80 or 220-27. No. 537-80 was manufactured in 1936 and was the twenty-ninth T-35 produced. No. 220-27 was also manufactured in 1936, but was the nineteenth T-35 produced.

Whatever the chassis number, the tank on the first T-35 features two strips of support armour on the turret, the late exhaust, the late driver's vision hatch, and amplified MG turret faces. The second tank shares all the same technical features of this tank with the exception of two key differences: the tank has a 'BT' style driver's access hatch and a solid front idler wheel. It is unclear which driver's hatch the first tank has, but it is more likely to have the standard early two-part hatch. If it does have the early two-part hatch, then this tank is in fact 220-27, but until further photographic evidence appears of both tanks, nothing is certain.

Both tanks served with the 68th Tank Regiment, and both were lost on 24 June 1941 in the village of Gorodok, which was being used as the repair centre for the 67th Tank Regiment. Both tanks have clear evidence of being under repair.

The first tank was lost next to a wooden house. The tank was probably under repair; however, the tank also shows signs of burning with discolouration on the rear fender and a blackened turret. It is possible that the tank was used as a static defence. However, it is far more likely that the Germans shot at the tank 'just in case' the tank was still active.

What is thought to be 220-27. Noteworthy features include the dislodged main turret (with clear evidence of burning), the late exhaust, and most intriguingly, a white '7' painted on the nose of the skirt. This is the only photograph with this feature known and is especially interesting as there were seven T-35s lost in Gorodok.

The same T-35A as in the previous image. Key features of this tank include the obvious damage to the tank, the state of disrepair, and the location of the tank. Compared to the tank opposite, it is easy to see that the tanks technical features are almost identical. This tank is more likely to be 220-27 due to the lack of certain technical features as mentioned.

What is thought to be 537-80. This tank is more likely to be T-35A 537-80 due to the technical features such as the solid drive wheel and the 'BT' style driver's access hatch. The position of the main turret is identical to the state of the tank in the background on page 83. However, this position also makes it look deceptively similar to the other T-35. Unfortunately, not visible here are the '=' divisional markings on the turret.

As strange as it may sound, this was a fairly common tactic as tanks would pretend to be knocked out before rumbling back to life and attacking the rear of the enemy with often devastating results.

The second T-35 was lost in the field of the repair centre, but a long way away from the other tanks. Apart from the 'BT' hatch, the other differences were the '=' mark painted onto the turret and a solid front idler wheel.

This T-35 remains a mystery. Noteworthy features include the dislodged main turret (with clear evidence of burning), the late exhaust, and most intriguingly, a white '7' painted on the nose of the skirt. There is only one known photograph displaying this feature; this is especially interesting as there were seven T-35s lost in Gorodok.

Unknown T-35A

One of the most mysterious T-35s, this tank so far only has five published photographs of it, all of them from the same angle depicting the almost same damage and condition. What is known and evident in the photographs is that it has a single-hatched turret with one strip of support on the turret, eight antenna feet, the late exhaust, and late driver's vision hatch. Also, note that the machine gun turret faces have amplification.

As to why these tanks are unknown, there is not enough photographic information to explain why or where these tanks were lost. Generally speaking, the tanks identified

One of only a handful of pictures of this vehicle. Unfortunately, there is not enough evidence to place this vehicle geographically or numerically. (*Vladimir Nemeshin*)

were done so by comparing the photographic record, with real locations and collating this with the table of losses.

Referencing the table of losses there are six T-35s that this tank could be: 339-48, 339-78, 288-43, 288-74, 183-5, and 183-7. All of these tanks would be single-turret-hatched T-35s with turrets that had one strip of support and eight antenna arms. This tank has so little known about it that there is nothing to reference it to the chassis table. This tank is more likely to be a tank from the 68th Tank Regiment as the '=' divisional marking is clearly seen. Therefore, chassis numbers 183-5, 339-68, and 288-74 are the most likely candidates to be this tank.

Unknown T-35A

Another unknown T-35A tank, this was produced between 1935 and 1936. When there is an unknown T-35 with a single turret hatch, the only way to tell roughly what production runs it could be is by looking at the turret. This T-35 has eight antenna arms, which rules out 148 chassis numbers, and one strip of support on the turret, which rules out 220 and 537 chassis numbers. Therefore, this tank could be a 339, 228, or 183 chassis number. Unfortunately, further deductions are hard to make.

Referencing the table of losses, there are six T-35s this tank could be: 339-48, 339-78, 288-43, 288-74, 183-5, and 183-7. All of these tanks would be single turret hatched T-35s, with turrets that had one strip of support and eight antenna arms. Of these, cross-referencing the lost tanks, the chassis numbers 183-7, 288-43, and 183-5 remain. This corresponds to the

The tank on 16 July 1941. Notice the late exhaust and the late placement of the stowage—the location of the wood saw. The damage on the antenna is also typical of this tank.

A rather beautiful photograph of this T-35. It is evident that this photograph was taken a long time after the tank was abandoned. It has been moved to the side of the road. The tracks have been removed and lie either side of the tank. Interestingly, the normal white paint for warning German drivers of the hazard has been accompanied with black paint. The armoured cap for one of the periscopes is still in place on the main turret periscope.

The same tank at a slightly later date, judging by the tank's condition. The antenna is missing from the left side of the turret. The track has been placed against the tank.

date that they were lost. Nos 183-7 and 288-65 were deployed on the 68th Tank Regiment, and are less likely to be this tank as it does not have the '=' mark on the turret. However, it does have the location of 'near Lviv'. Nos 288-43 and 183-5 are a part of the 67th Tank Regiment; of these two, only 183-5 has a location of 'near Lviv'. It therefore is likely to be this tank, but until more information is gathered, it is hard to make a definitive decision.

Some speculation is that this tank could be 183-5, which was simply labelled 'lost outside of Lviv' in the losses of the 67th and 68th Tank Regiments. While the chassis number is unknown, it is known that the tank was abandoned on the modern H17 road travelling east, just outside of Hamaliivka, which in turn, is next to Zapytiv, where 234-42 was abandoned. The modern E40 highway now starts roughly where this tank was abandoned, just within 20 miles of Lviv. Again, it is only speculated that this T-35 is 183-5.

The tank displays a mix of features including the late exhaust, the late stowage with the wood saw next to the rear machine gun turret and the machine gun turret faces are without amplification.

Unknown T-35A

This tank is just another of the many T-35s that have not been identified with a chassis number. The features of this tank include one strip of support armour, eight antenna feet, amplified MG turret faces, the late exhaust, and the late driver's vision hatch.

Regarding the table of losses there are six T-35s this tank could be: 339-48, 339-78, 288-43, 288-74, 183-5, and 183-7. All of these tanks would be single turret hatched T-35s, with turrets that had one strip of support and eight antenna arms. Of these, cross referencing the documents of lost tanks leaves the chassis numbers 183-7, 288-43, and 183-5.

This photo is grainy; however, the branch attached to the KT-28 gun is confirmed with other photographs of the same tank. This tank also appears to not have the red star, a normal feature of T-35s. An interesting note is the state of the tracks, with the metallic shine of the teeth. This photo was taken some time after abandonment as the armaments (machine guns) and optics have been removed.

The tank was left on the road only for a short time before it was moved to the side of the road. While at first glance it might be hard to collate the two pictures with each other, this tank had both metal traps at the rear for attaching the fender to the skirt removed, clearly visible in both pictures. The German soldiers give a real sense of scale with the return rollers for the track being almost 2 m above the ground. The obvious tactical disadvantages are huge as the tank was an obvious target.

Almost no information on this T-35 exists as all photographs of it simply depict it on a dirt road. The tank was covered in branches to camouflage the tank. This was simply an impossible task as the tank was so large.

Unknown T-35A

Probably the most famous T-35 in this publication is the T-35 that served at Moscow. However, considering its relative popularity, there is very little known about the tank. It appears in only two published propaganda pictures and at unfavourable angles at that. It also appears in a newly published picture; however, using the table of production, it can be narrowed down to a small group of tanks.

Of the tanks not listed in the documentation of the 67th and 68th Tank Regiments, plus those tanks listed at Kharkiv, there are no fewer than eight vehicles this tank could be. Of these, this tank cannot be 0197-7 as that tank has survived to this day; it is preserved at the Kubinka Tank Museum. This tank came from the Saratov Tank School.

This leaves the following chassis numbers: 148-11, 148-19, 148-31,148-40, 148-41, 288-41, and 988-18. Comparing these numbers with the T-35 pictures, the tank does not appear to be equipped with a P-40 AA mount. This rules out 988-18.

The turret does not appear to have a second support strip on the turret. In other pictures of the tank, the foot plates for the arms seem to be misshapen and too large, indicating that it was replaced. These features are consistent with a 148 chassis number. The tank is equipped with the updated exhaust. This feature was shared by almost every T-35.

While speculation, it is fair to assume it was a 148 chassis number, if for nothing else than the majority of the chassis numbers that this tank could be are 148 chassis numbers. There is another known T-35 in photographs—the second T-35 at Saratov that was used in the film *Battle Before Moscow*. This too appears to be a 148 chassis number tank. Interestingly, this tank and the tank at Saratov are the only known T-35s still to be equipped with combat lights.

Unknown T-35A

The T-35s that served at the Saratov Tank School had an uneventful but important role in the war—for training tank crews. However, one tank was used for the propaganda role. This tank was filmed at Saratov for the propaganda film *Battle Before Moscow*.

While the exact chassis number is not known, it is known that the tank has one hatch in the turret and one strip of support on the turret. In addition to this, it is equipped with the updated exhaust system. In the film, the tank is still painted green and lacks an antenna; however, the tank, like the one at Moscow, has combat lights on the 76-mm gun. Interestingly, the periscopes were equipped with the early square covers.

It is not known what happened to this tank, whether it was scrapped or sent to the front. Nevertheless, apart from its role in the film *Battle Before Moscow*, no other evidence exists of this tank.

Even in 1941, the T-35 was still playing the important propaganda role. The tank is actually in the suburbs of Moscow with militia soldiers. The tank has not been whitewashed yet. It appears in two famous propaganda photographs from Moscow, whitewashed in both. (*Maxim Kolomiets*)

A propaganda picture from Saratov. This T-35 has combat lights, one of only two confirmed to still be equipped with them during the war. (*Maxim Kolomiets*)

Unknown T-35A

This tank is another of the unknown T-35s. However, unlike most, this tank has two support strips on the turret rather than one. The technical features include the late exhaust, single turret hatch, two support strips, a solid front idler wheel, and a 'BT' style driver's access hatch.

Referencing the table of losses, there are only two T-35s this tank could be: 220-29 or 220-43. These tanks have single turret hatches with two strip of support and eight antenna arms. Not much is known about this tank; however, it could be 220-29 as this tank shares many of the features that 220-25 was equipped with. If so, the tank was bogged down and was left near Sudova Vyshnia.

Unknown T-35A

An unknown T-35A tank and the first T-35 in this book with a P-40 AA mount. The technical features include the late driver's vision hatch, the late exhaust, and unamplified machine gun turrets. It is unknown exactly when this T-35 was manufactured; however, it was certainly between the years 1937 and 1938.

While the actual T-35 chassis number is not known, pieces of information are available. This tank likely served with the 68th Tank Regiment, and was lost with T-35 744-62 in the village of Gorodok. The tank ended up in a ditch in the road opposite a political building. Interestingly, 744-62 appears to have been towed or, at least, towing was attempted. All T-35s lost in Gorodok were lost on 24 June 1941.

Referencing the table of losses with T-35s not identified, this tank could be 217-35. However, this is only because it is one of the few unidentified P-40 mount tanks. 217-35 'bogged down' with no date or location. One suggestion is that this tank was updated with a P-40 AA mount; a suggestion for chassis numbers then is 288-43 due to the date.

Attempts to identify the chassis number have proven to be fruitless. The only T-35 that has an outside chance of being this is 0200-8. This is only due to the date of loss on 26 June.

T-35A 148-22 (Updated)

T-35A 148-22 was made in 1934 and was the third T-35 built, making it the earliest T-35 in this publication and the earliest known T-35 identified. It started life as an initial production T-35, with the single turret hatch and six antenna arms. However, it would be returned to the factory for some experimental upgrades in the late 1930s in Kharkiv.

Its technical features included machine gun turret amplification, late exhaust, and a P-40 AA mount in the turret—by far the most fascinating feature. This was one of two T-35s that were updated with P-40 mounts from the old single hatch. The original foot plates, unlike other T-35s, have been completely removed with no evidence of their original position. This was also the case for 148-25's and 148-30's rear two foot plates.

Only five photos of this tank seem to exist. Most of these are rather blurry; subsequently, not much is known about the tank compared to others. What is known is that it was lost

The Combat Debut of the T-35A Tank in Photos

The same tank, however, with a large group of Germans using the tank as a good photograph spot. The tank is basically in the same position as the previous photograph.

This image clearly shows the tank's modernised features, such as the solid front idler wheel and the 'BT' style driver's hatch. Also, the red stars have been covered over with paint.

The tank in the ditch in August 1941. The theory that this tank was towing 744-62 could be true as this photo indicates the tow eye missing on the rear right eye and the rope along the rear of the tank.

The same T-35A as in the previous pages. In the background is T-35 744-62. This conical T-35 is in the exact same condition as shown on page 118. Also note the antenna, which is partly missing; the left side is gone, whereas the right is complete. The red brick political building is visible in this photograph; it still exists, but it has since been converted into flats.

This photograph was taken at a later date to the previous photograph as indicated by the state of the antenna on the turret. The arms on the right are still intact, but the actual aerial is missing. Note the late stowage. Interestingly, the tank has managed to retain one of the transmission access hatches, which was very rare for a T-35.

A closer look at this T-35's nose and forward turrets. On the inside of the 45-mm gun turret, the top of an ammunition rack can be seen. There were three racks inside this turret, plus a machine gun ammunition magazine. Interestingly, this tank is devoid of a horn.

The snow had begun to fall on Gorodok. It is entirely unknown how long these tanks sat in the positions they were lost in before being broken up or recaptured by the Russians. There is no evidence in the west that these giants were recaptured, and some photographs exist of these tanks in a very late stage of dismantlement.

in a field and seems to have been knocked out during combat. All photos show the tank in a blown-up state, but importantly, the turret is facing rearwards, possibly indicating the tank was engaging a target at its rear.

Interestingly, the location of the tank has been identified as near the town of Sasiv, but closer to the village of Khmeleva. It is thought this tank was also lost in the fighting for Sasiv. Based on the location, leading T-35 experts have identified the tank as 148-22 as the records of the 68th Tank Regiment describe 148-22 as being lost 'in Sasiv'. Even with the often fairly inaccurate records, this was actually fairly close to the actual location of the tank in a field near Sasiv.

The front 45-mm gun hatch has a strip of metal separating the left and right access hatches (both of which are completely missing). The front of the fender is missing. This is not the only T-35 missing this part; T-35A 0200-9 is also missing this on the left side.

There is some contention that another T-35 with a P-40 AA mount with one strip of support exists. The pictures show a tank very similar to this one, and so it is unclear if it is the same vehicle; however, the damage does appear slightly different, thus indicating a different vehicle.

T-35A 148-25 (Updated)

T-35A 148-25 was manufactured in 1934 and was the fourth T-35 produced. Almost at the same time as 148-22, this tank was returned to the factory (likely in 1938 due to it

T-35A 148-22. (*Vladimir Nemeshin*)

featuring the late driver's vision hatch) and was re-equipped in an attempt to update the older tanks to the newer standard.

Its features include the late driver's vision hatch, amplification of the MG turret faces, the late driver's access hatch, the late exhaust, a P-40 AA mount, and a single strip of support on the turret. As the same as the previous tank, this vehicle was upgraded from a single turret hatch to the P-40 AA mount after production.

The tank was issued to the 68th Tank Regiment and was lost in the village of Staryi Yarychiv, which is the next village along the E40 highway east from Zapytiv (where 234-42 was lost). It was this feature that identified this vehicle as 148-25, as the records describe 148-25 as being lost in Zapytiv. According to the table of losses, 234-42 was lost on 3 July, although this is inaccurate as the location was captured on 29 June.

This tank was lost due to enemy action. It was retreating eastward, driving though the village Staryi Yarychiv. It had just driven past the Staryi Yarychiv cemetery, which was towards the brewery and the exit of the village. The main turret was facing rearward, possibly engaging or looking for targets. The tank, however, was hit at least once from fire from the north (on the left of the tank from the driver's perspective). This appears to have ignited the tank and detonated the canister of compressed gas in the smoke generator, which, in turn, blew out the smoke generator's side.

Inspecting the tank, burn and scorch marks can be clearly seen around the exit points of the tank, including the 45-mm gun turret's vision ports. It is unknown if the crew were killed, captured, or managed to escape. However, it is most likely that the crew were killed. The tank sat in its position; it was lost in for a fair amount of time before being moved roughly 50 m up the road to a position outside of a house. This house was simply a peasant's house and had severe damage to the roof, which was burned off. The tank was systematically stripped of parts, including the track and skirts. At the same time, the

T-35A 715-61

T-35A 715-61 was the first T-35A to be factory-produced with a P-40 AA mount. The tank was made in 1936 and was the thirty-first T-35 produced. The tank's technical features include the late driver's vision and entrance hatch and the late exhaust. The tank was issued to the 68th Tank Regiment when the war broke out. The tank was lost in the village of Sudova Vyshnia on 24 June 1941 due to gearbox failure.

This tank was one of the most recently identified tanks, along with 988-17. Leading experts on T-35s agree that this tank was most likely lost in the Ukrainian village of Sudova Vyshnia (*Судова Вишня*). This village was the location of the 68th Tank Regiment's repair centre and was also the next town along from Gorodok, the repair centre for the 67th Tank Regiment. Photographs of this tank show it lost next to a fence and two cottages. There is a road behind the tank that has not yet been identified.

The tank faced south with photographs of the hills in front of the tank clearly visible. The tank was seen in this position for the remainder of the war, slowly being stripped of parts over time. It is known that the antenna was removed fully leaving just the arms in January 1942 as the photographic evidence depicts this.

T-35A 715-62

T-35A 715-62 was the second T-35A produced with a P-40 AA mount, the last T-35 manufactured in 1936, and the thirty-second T-35 produced. The tank's technical features included the late driver's vision hatch, the late exhaust, and the complete removal of the clothes line antenna, leaving only the foot plates intact.

This tank was delivered to the 68th Tank Regiment in June 1941 and was lost on 29 June 1941 within Lviv as a result of the engine cooling fan failing. In the photos of the tank in Lviv, the fan cover has been unbolted from the hinges and is lying loose on the fan deck.

The current location of the tank would be Zaliznychna Street. This road runs parallel to the railway line in the north-west of the city. It is now a cobbled road that is a construction site. The building behind the tank was still standing in 2005; however, it has since been demolished. Further along the railway line, there is a road bridge, this is Levandivska Street.

This would normally be where tanks stayed until they were destroyed or scrapped. However, 715-62 was selected by the OKH (*Oberkommando des Heeres*) to be returned to Germany for inspection. The tank was driven by the Germans to a park about 100 m north of its abandonment location. There, it was loaded onto a train bound for Berlin.

The tank was shipped to the Kummersdorf Proving Grounds, which was home to the Kummersdorf Captured Equipment Centre in the suburbs of Berlin. There, measurements of armour thickness were taken and marked in white numbers on each part of the tank. It was also photographed in great detail. The tank stayed at Kummersdorf for the rest of

The next four photographs were taken by the same soldier on the same day, either the day that it was lost, or the day after. There are scorch marks on the 45-mm gun turret alongside the '=' divisional markings on the turret.

This photograph clearly shows the combat damage—the tank having been hit by a shot from the north as the tank was moving eastwards. Note the equipment on the engine deck, including a spare road wheel and what looks like a spare exhaust pipe (or conversely a suspension spring in a case). The tow eye on the fender is next to the turret pedestal and the late exhaust.

Another photo of this same tank. From this angle, it is clear that the transmission hatches have been removed. The two ladders seen on the fenders were typically stowed here. Interestingly, there are no tow eyes on the attachments at the rear of the tank.

The last photograph of 148-25 from the set with the previous pictures. There are burn marks on the tank around the vision slits of the front 45-mm gun. Interestingly, note the unusual placing of the front tow rope crossing over the front of the tank and the top of the 45-mm gun turret. The air filtration port is open. This simply was a hole in the turret roof to help air circulation as firing the gun created toxic smoke that could disorientate crewmen.

A long amount of time has passed since the last four photographs; now the tank has been moved down the road and it has been stripped of parts. There is an engineer with a blow torch behind the two officers. Interestingly, a hole from a shell is visible between the two brackets of the right jack on the smoke generator. In this picture, the roof of the cottage is being rethatched, having the 'A' beams in place. The tank was abandoned a short while down from the village cemetery. Some photos also show the brewery.

One of the more common T-35s to be photographed, 715-61 sits in a small field next to a couple of houses in the small yet important village of Sudova Vsyhnia.

The following five photographs were taken by a talented photographer from the 257 Infantry Division in early 1941, likely taken at the time of the vehicles capture. Here, 715-61 sits where it was abandoned, never to move again. There is a strange tool box in front of the lights. Many little features of the tank can be seen on this photograph, including the strange partition in the MG turrets inner cheek. There was no vision port and it is unknown why this is here.

A rare front view of 715-61. There is damage to the front fender and, interestingly, the ball mount rear MG.

The Combat Debut of the T-35A Tank in Photos

A rare view of the top of a T-35. On the rear MG turret can be seen a Russian tank helmet and the gas recoiling system for a DT-29 machine gun. Strange white-bottomed bricks can be seen on the rear 45-mm gun turret and the rear MG position. There are the holes from small arms fire on the turret. This was likely when the German first found the tank and shot at it 'just to make sure'. Pay close attention to the details on the turret, turret roof, and even inside the 45-mm gun turret.

One of the key features of this tank is that the antenna has damaged. The front arm is broken, likely in conjunction with the small arms fire that this tank clearly received. A common defect with the T-35s was the build-up of mud around the drive wheel, clearly seen here. This was such a serious issue that later tanks had redesigned skirts to fix this issue.

The last photograph from this collection. The ball mount for the rear MG turret is wedged between the rear turret and the guard to stop the MG from shooting the rear of the tank. The gas replicating system for this gun is missing and is found on the roof of the MG turret in previous photographs. The two ladders were normally stowed onto the rear of the tank's fenders.

Above: No. 715-61. Notice the late exhaust and the damage to the antenna.

Below: Interestingly, these photos appear to have been taken by a soldier in the 24th Flak Regiment. He was quite accurate with locations as labelled on the back of his photographs, with this T-35 being labelled in the village of Sudova Vyshnia. The same soldier took the photograph of 0200-4 on page 101.

This photograph appears to be from the same photographer as the previous two pictures. (*Sergey Lotarev*)

No. 715-61, most likely a few months later than the earlier photographs. The P-40 AA mount and the clothes line antenna is missing the first arm (but otherwise is complete). Also note the amplified MG turret armour. In addition, the late driver's hatch is hinged together rather than on separate sides. Later on, in 1942, the antenna was completely removed from the tank along with the track.

Above left: No. 715-61 in Kummersdorf. This was an estate roughly 25 km outside of Berlin. It was the location of the German site for evaluation of captured equipment. Within this compound, captured tanks were weighed, armour thickness was tested, and German troops and officers were allowed to inspect the tanks for recognition in the field. In this photograph, 'T-35A' has been written on the inside left fender. On the right, there is a wooden set of steps leading to the tank for access. This was also a major issue with the tank for Russians as the tank was rather high.

Above right: No. 715-61 in Kummersdorf. There is a BT-7 Model 1935 next to it. Many captured tanks from all nations were displayed at Kummersdorf and all were used in the final days of the war.
One photograph exists of 715-62 in 1945 after being used by the Germans. The photograph in question was taken by the Commander of the 22nd Motorised Brigade on 22 April 1945. The tank does not have any tracks, skirts, or guns. It is suggested that it was being used as an observation post.

Below: No. 715-62 in Lvov, July 1941. The rear fan cover is not attached to the tank. Also note the position of the P-40 AA mount; the mount could in fact rotate as it was also attached to an anti-aircraft gun (7.62-mm DT-29) in a ball mount on an arm that could also be raised or lowered.

the war, until 1945 when it was used by the Wehrmacht. This particular tank appears in the German technical manual for Tiger tanks issued to crews. It is listed as an obsolete type and has the armour thickness measurements marked.

Several photos exist of the tank on display in a hall or in a courtyard with many other tanks including T-28s, T-34s, T-26s, and BT tanks. The tank was listed with vehicles in use by the Wehrmacht in Berlin in 1945; one photograph exists of the tank outside Berlin being used as an observation platform.

T-35A 0197-1

T-35A 0197-1 was the first T-35 produced in 1937 and was the thirty-third T-35 produced. Interestingly, the chassis numbers of this tank were manufactured in two batches, both at the beginning of the year; 0197-1 and 0197-6 were both manufactured in 1937, and 0197-2 and 0197-7 were both manufactured in 1938. The tanks technical features include the early driver's vision hatch, the late exhaust, and MG turrets without amplification.

This tank served with the 67th Tank Regiment at the outbreak of the Second World War, and has the distinction of not only being the first T-35 lost in the war, but the first T-35 lost due to a technical issue rather than to combat.

According to the records, the tank was lost on 25 June 1941. This tank was abandoned between the villages of Pidberiztsi and Chyzhykiv (now on the modern E40 highway). These villages are 20 km to the east of Lviv. Interestingly, this was way behind the German front line, but it was not recoverable in the situation of the opening days of war, so the tank was lost.

This tank was to sit on this road well into 1942. The tank has its clothes line antenna removed in early 1942, before the tank was recovered by the Germans; it was then moved to a German training area in Ukraine.

The T-35 had a captured tank Panzer number—Pz.Kpfw. 751(r). The tank was used in an infantry AT (anti-tank) training role, being set on fire and driven around. Not much is known about its job role whilst serving the Germans. Other tanks were used in a similar role; however, they were used in the position they were lost in. Nos 148-50, 196-94, and 0200-4 were all utilised by the Germans as training tanks; however, they were used only once and all were partly or totally blown up.

T-35A -197-6

This tank is another more recently identified T-35. No. 0197-6 was manufactured in 1937, and was the thirty-fourth T-35 produced. The tank is issued with the late exhaust, early driver's vision hatch, and unamplified MG turrets.

The documentation of this tank described it as 'dead batteries' near the town of Dzerdzuno. This is claimed to have happened on 9 July, but was more likely 3–5 July. The photographic evidence, however, suggests it was bogged down after being forced off the road.

When inspecting this tank, consider why the tank drove of the clearly visible road, and the debris from other vehicles around it. Perhaps this tank was attacked by aircraft and

For a German soldier marching to the front, the summer of 1941 would have been a photographic dream, with so many abandoned Russian tanks to explore and photograph. Here, 0197-1 sits on the road on 1 July 1941. Truly a fallen giant, the tank strikes a fitting pose. Even though the tank is large, the turrets are noticeably small. The German soldier gives an interesting perspective for the few crew squeezed into the turrets. This tank has the redesigned stowage layout with the wood saw next to the radiator intake and the ladders are seen on the rear fender.

The guns have been played with, changing position from the previous photograph; it was very common for this to happen. It is one of the main ways of following the sequence of photographs from early 1941 to as late as mid-1943. Notice the pistol port with the plug attached with a metal chain.

No. 0197-1 sits where it was lost in mid-1941. The P-40 AA mount is obscured, and without it, the tank looks very similar to another T-35 with a single turret hatch on page 57. However, the shape of the rear antenna matches up with photos of 0197-1. The nurse on the tank is German.

Above: No. 0197-1 from the front. The early-type driver's vision hatch and access hatch are both evident. The tank is missing the horn; there appears to be several examples of T-35 without their horns. This tank was one of a handful of T-35s used by the Wehrmacht. This tank was moved to a training centre in Ukraine and used as a mobile target for infantry AT training. On the skirt side was written '*Keine Munition Verwenden!*' ('Do not use ammunition!')

Below: T-35A chassis number 0197-1. This is the earliest of the three photographs as the tank still has the jacks attached to the smoke generator side.

No. 0197-6 a short while after the abandonment of the tank. The damage sustained to the tank includes the removal of two of the skirt to fender attachment points at the rear of the fender. In addition, the mud on the tank has reached to the top of the skirt, implying the tank drove in deep mud before bogging down.

drove off the road to avoid bombs. What is clear is that the crew had enough time to try to salvage the tank, with the screw to tighten the track clearly seen in some photographs.

T-35A 196-94

One of two experimental T-35s, 196-94 was the thirty-sixth T-35 produced and was an attempt to improve upon the T-35 tank. After the summer manoeuvres of 1936, reports were made on the performance of the T-35s. Crews were not happy with the tank as it was prone to breakdown, engine and transmission failures, and the track would often be pushed off of the drive wheel by a build-up of mud behind the skirt.

Therefore, in 1937, the KhPZ produced two experimental hulls with improvements to the tank. The tanks skirts were shortened to leave the drive wheel exposed. Access ports were cut into the skirt from the rear of the skirt and reached as far forward as the third skirt plate. There were no metal straps attaching the skirt to the fender, and thicker metal strips attached each part of the fender together. The turret pedestal was redesigned to incorporate the smoke generators into the pedestal, rather than boxes attached to the tank. This gave the turret a hexagonal shape.

While these upgrades were indeed improvements, only two tanks were manufactured before production switched back to the normal hulls. However, this hull would later be reused on the conical-turreted T-35s.

Above and below: The same tank once again in the above two photographs. From the front, features like the late driver's vision hatch is clearly visible. It is unknown why the tank drove off the road; perhaps air attack is to blame. The BT-7 behind the tank has a clothes line antenna.

Below: This T-35 was lost on a road heading east and got stuck in mud at the side of the road. The tank sat here for the rest of the war. It is interesting to note the hinged gun replicator armour on the main KT-28 gun. The object in the foreground is unknown; however, it could have something to do with the power lines in the background that follow parallel to the road.

No. 196-94 after being used by the Germans for AT training. Notice the inspection ports in the hull and the skirt cut-off point. In the foreground, an M-17L aero engine sits. This engine powered many Soviet vehicles, including the T-35, the BT-7, and the T-34. (*Sergey Lotarev*)

No. 196-94 had all the features described, including the late exhaust system and the late driver's hatch. In 1941, it was issued to the 68th Tank Regiment and had an '=' divisional marking painted onto the turret.

When war broke out, the tank was under capital repairs in Sudova Vyshnia, the repair centre for the 68th Tank Regiment. Here, it was captured on 24 June 1941.

Just like 148-50 and 0200-4, the tank was used by the Germans for infantry AT training. The tank was blown up by the Germans very early in July 1941, and photos of the tank while still intact are hard to come by. The tank appears to have spent the rest of the war a smashed pile of scrap in Sudova Vyshnia

Gorodok Repair Centre
196-95, 744-64, 339-75, and 537-80/220-27

The repair yard in Gorodok is known to have held the following tanks: 196-95, 744-64, 339-75, and an unknown chassis number (known to be either 220-27 or 537-80).

No. 196-95 was one of the experimental T-35s built with a hybrid chassis. The hull skirt access panels to the running gear was unique to chassis 196-94 and 196-95. While these are a steeper angle to the other later tanks' skirt access panels, the chassis was basically identical to any tank with chassis numbers 234 or 744 up until 744-63. There were also holes in the skirt and pedestal. There is some footage of this tank being shot at by a Pak 38 50-mm gun; the Germans were probably testing the tank's armour thickness.

No. 744-64 was the first T-35 conical produced with the square access ports in the hull. The tank is outwardly identical to 744-67. It had a solid front idler wheel and the

'BT' style driver's hatch. This was implemented on the last four T-35s produced and tanks returning to the factory in Kharkiv. Other tanks with this hatch include 537-70.

No. 339-75 was a single turret-hatched T-35A with amplification on the MG turret faces. This tank was in a very similar state as 148-50, with most of the engine deck removed. This tank is famous for having German inscriptions describing how many guns it was equipped with.

The other T-35 was either 537-80 or 220-27. The 'BT' style driver's access hatch is visible in some photographs. The tank had the '=' divisional markings on the turret. Interestingly, both 220-27 and 537-80 belonged to the 68th Tank Regiment, whereas the other tanks belonged to the 67th Tank Regiment. It is unknown why these two tanks were also lost here; however, Gorodok being used as a repair yard probably has something to do with it.

This repair yard was not quite so empty; all of the 67th Tank Regiment's T-37A amphibious tanks were left along with these T-35s. They used the same type of wooden jig used to remove engines as is seen in many photos of T-35s in repair yards.

All of these tanks were abandoned in the town of Gorodok (modern day Horodok), about 150 m south of the other two T-35s lost in the town—744-62 and an unknown P-40 AA mount tank. This area is now an urban built up area. The grass area that the tanks were on is behind Gorodok cemetery, the tree line behind the tanks is the rear of the cemetery. Originally, the entrance to this grass was next to where 744-62 was lost. Up to seven tanks were lost in Gorodok; six tanks have been vigorously documented and the last tank has only one existing close up image published of it (the rear tank).

The Gorodok Repair Centre and the base for the 67th Tank Regiment. Stretching into the distance is no fewer than four T-35s: 196-95, 744-64, 339-75, and what is believed to be 537-80. Notice there is an Yugoslavian soldier in the foreground; although highly unusual, it is not uncommon.

T-35A 196-96

T-35A 196-96 was manufactured in 1937, and was the thirty-seventh T-35 manufactured. The most interesting feature with 196-96 is that it was a part of the production run that implemented the new prototype chassis, but was manufactured with the standard hull.

The tank's technical features include the standard hull, the late exhaust, and the late driver's vision hatch. The tank was issued to the 68th Tank Regiment, and was the last T-35 to be lost in the 68th Tank Regiment on 2 July 1941.

The tank was lost due to final drive failure, just outside Ternopil, in the village of Kutkivtsi, within the Ternopil boundary. The tank would have currently lay on the H-02 highway, L'vivs'ka St, directly outside the Ternopil Economic University.

Originally lost a few metres up the road from this location, very early on after capture, the tank was moved backwards to the more common position to find it in.

T-35A 988-15

T-35A 988-15 was manufactured in 1937 and was the thirty-eighth T-35 produced. The 988's technical features were quite interesting; this late into production, they were issued with very early features. These include the early exterior type exhaust pipe and the early driver's vision hatch; however, 988-15 had a solid front idler wheel.

This tank was issued to the 68th Tank Regiment, however was not issued with the '=' divisional markings. Instead the crew were ordered to paint a white '14' on the smoke generator. The tank was lost on 2 July 1941 in Zolochiv along with a T-28. The tank was lost due to gearbox failure. Originally, the tank was lost in the proximity of the Zolochiv Cemetery; however, some point in late 1941, it was moved north opposite two thatched cottages. It sat there, with the T-28Eh, for the remainder of the war.

T-35A 988-16

T-35A 988-16 was manufactured in 1937 and was the thirty-ninth T-35 produced. This tank shared the same technical features as her sisters; this includes the early driver's vision hatch and the early exterior type exhaust. However, unlike her sister 988-15, this T-35 has the early 'spider' or 'webbed' idler wheel.

This T-35 was issued to the 68th Tank Regiment, and was one of four T-35s that was involved in the Battle of Verba on 30 June 1941. The tank—along with 148-39, 220-25, 0200-0, and 988-16—attacked the German 16th Panzer Division at the village of Verba. The other three tanks were all lost at the eastern entrance of the village, however it would appear the 988-16 managed to fight its way through the village. Some of the only confirmed kills of T-35s were in the battle, and undoubtedly 988-16 had a role to play in this.

Two Panzer IIIs were lost on the eastern entrance to the village; however, it is unknown what else was lost. No. 988-16 appears to have made it through the village of Verba to the west side along with a single T-26 before it, too, was brought to a halt by enemy fire. It is

The Combat Debut of the T-35A Tank in Photos

No. 196-96 shortly after the tank was lost. This photograph was taken before the tank was moved back down the road. The jack is still in the bracket. Also, the damage to the fender just below the smoke generator is evident in later photographs.

No. 196-96 after the tank was moved backwards to its final location. The jack bracket is now home to a sign post. The post is pointing north-west back towards the E-40 highway towards Lviv.

No. 196-96, most likely later than the previous photo. The direction sign between the two brackets has been moved and appears to have fallen. From this angle, the late driver's vision hatch and the divisional '=' sign that is painted on the turret can be seen. The red star is on the skirt and there is damage to the fender. This was the last tank from the 68th Tank Regiment that was lost. The small village in the background is Kutkivtsi, a village within the Ternopil boundary. The tank would have currently lay on the H-02 highway, directly outside the Ternopil Economic University.

No. 988-15 after it was moved from its original spot to further south down the road. Take note of the technical features of this tank—the solid front idler wheel is clearly visible, along with the cover for the early exhaust pipe. Also, the tank does not have the amplification on the MG turrets. The white '14' is just visible on the smoke generator.

The original location of 988-15 when it was abandoned in Zolochiv. It is unknown how many times the tank was moved, either once or twice; however, the T-28 is not in view here. This implies either the T-28 moved or 988-15 moved. Interestingly, the position that the tank was moved to later and had its tracks removed is visible in this picture. The tank was dragged up the road to a position about 20 m south of the houses in the rear of this picture.

The German *schwein*. The original location of the two tanks next to the large building, which itself is opposite the building in the background of the next photograph. While the T-28 takes prominence in the picture, 988-15 is visible behind it. The GAZ truck is missing a wheel in the foreground as well. This is not evident in other pictures of this tank at the same time.

No. 988-15 from the front. From this view, the T-28 and buildings in the background are much clearer. On the T-35 itself, the early driver's vision hatch and the two part early driver's escape hatch are visible. This T-28 was manufactured in 1936 and upgraded in 1940 with additional armour plates. The brick building with the chimney in the background on the right was the original location of 988-15 when it was lost. This building still exists and was the defining building used in identifying the location of the tank. This building is opposite Zolochiv's old cemetery.

T-35 988-15 and the T-28 were moved north between 50 m and 100 m to this position. The track was partly removed and curled up as seen here.

This T-35 was lost on a road heading east and got stuck in mud at the side of the road. The tank sat here for the rest of the war. In the above photo, it is interesting to note the hinged gun replicator armour on the main KT-28 gun. The object in the foreground is unknown; however, it could have something to do with the powerlines in the background that follow parallel to the road.

unknown where and when it sustained hits during the battle; however, the photographic evidence paints a desperate fight to the end.

The first things that is noticeable is the damage to the turret, immediately indicating an internal explosion. The ball MG mount was blown out of the tank, the gun was knocked out of its cradle, and the clothes line antenna suffered damage. Next in the list of damage sustained is the front MG turret sustained such damage that the turret face was completely removed. The actual face has not been found. It is possible that the tank lost this earlier in the battle and continued on, or it was blown off when the main turret also blew. In addition to this, the front and sides of the tank are peppered with low calibre hits that mostly reflect 37-mm or 50-mm hits. These shots would have easily penetrated the thin 30-mm frontal armour of a T-35; however, most shots are concentrated around the turrets. Interestingly, the front 45-mm gun turret's periscope was completely removed by a shot, and it would appear that the front MG turret took a hit on the side that did not penetrate.

All in all, the tank sustained a hail of fire. This is not surprising, as the tank is a huge target, and missing this beast would be a hard job. The fact that the tank did take so many hits before succumbing is a testament to the tenacity of the crew. While the tank was not actually a modern of efficient fighting vehicle, it was still able to perform for some short engagements. This tank was filmed for the German propaganda film *Die Deutche Wochenshau*, with people inspecting ammunition, close ups of the MG turret face, and the front of this tank. The episode in question is No. 567, broadcast 16 July 1941; this tank appears just after the 0200-9.

T-35A 988-17

No. 988-17 was manufactured in 1937 and was the fortieth T-35 produced. This tank, again, shares similar features as her sisters such as the early exhaust, and driver's vision hatch. However, this T-35 had a much more extensive removal of the antenna on the turret. This tank is one of the most recent tanks identified by leading experts in the field, along with 715-62. No. 988-17 was lost on 29 June 1941. This tank was lost in the village of Sukhovolya ('*суховоля*'), which is on the L11 highway, to the west of Lviv.

It was originally thought to be either chassis numbers 988-17 or 715-62, as both tanks were lost on the same day (according to the combat reports) at around the same location; however recently conformation between leading figures in the T-35 history agreed and independently confirmed that this tank was 988-17. The dates seems to be very rough on the combat reports, as 715-61 was actually lost on 24 June.

0197-7: The Survivor

The last surviving T-35 had a rather mundane career. No. 0197-7 was manufactured in 1938 and was the forty-third T-35 manufactured. Unlike the majority of the vehicles on this list, the tank was not deployed in a combat role and was instead deployed with the Saratov Tank School. Saratov was equipped with five tanks at the beginning of the war, and it would appear that they all stayed at the training site. Saratov was never captured by German forces; the closest city captured was Stalingrad. It is unknown what actually happened to the tanks at Saratov; it is possible that the other four tanks were sent to the front in 1942. One of the other T-35s from Saratov was used in the film *Battle For Moscow* in 1941. This was likely one of the 148 chassis numbers.

Whatever their fate, the only T-35 left at the end of the war was 0197-7. It was sent to Kubinka in 1946, where pictures are available of the tank alongside panthers. She then became a part of the collection at Kubinka when it opened as a museum. In 2012, it was restored to running condition by wargaming.net for the video game *War Thunder*. It has been driven around at shows, but spends most of its time at Kubinka. It should be noted that the collection at Kubinka has now been split between 'Patriot Park' and Kubinka. The T-35 is at Kubinka alongside the surviving SU-14-1 and the T-100Y.

It should be noted a replica T-35 was constructed for the Uralmarch Tank Museum. While outwardly accurate, there are many flaws in this replica. However, the tank is a single-hatched turreted tank with two strips of support on the turret and the early exhaust.

T-35A 0200-0

T-35A 0200-0 is a standard P-40 AA mount tank manufactured in 1938. This tank was the forty-fifth T-35 produced. Technical features include the late driver's hatch, late exhaust, amplification on the MG turrets, and a total removal of the clothes line antenna.

Above: No. 988-16 after the Battle of Verba. The damage is very serious, with the ball mount on the main turret completely removed and lying on the ground. All the hits are to the front of the tank.

Below: With German trucks still burning, the wreck of 988-16 sits abandoned after the furious fighting at Verba. Just after the burning trucks, the road curves to the left, gradually heading down hill. If it was not for the wreck of 988-16, T-35A 220-25 would just be in view. (*Sergey Lotarev*)

German graves left after the battle are overshadowed by the slain monster that is 988-16. It is unknown which regiment the Germans belonged to. There is no evidence so far to any Russian graves; however, two full crews of T-35s (eleven men each) are known to have died, plus likely many other crew members from the other tanks were lost. (*Sergey Lotarev*)

T-35A 988-16 from the same collection as the previous photo. The T-35 was a very photogenic tank, and was very popular with the German soldiers. Almost out of view, there are five graves, all with helmets on them. These fallen Germans were killed in the fighting on 30 June 1941, in which this tank was knocked out. It is uncertain how many Russians were lost, but at least two full crews were killed, eleven men per tank (220-25 and 148-30).

Likely taken on 30 June or 1 July, this photograph of 988-16 has been annotated by the author. 'Kanone' simply means cannon, therefore indicating the location of a gun. This was possibly the gun that finally silenced 988-16. The fact that one of her guns, the front 45-mm gun, is trained towards that side of the road, and that the damage to the turret is from the right of the vehicle, indicates that this gun indeed stopped the last giant at Verba. The Sd.Kfz. 8 was used for towing heavy guns like Flak 88s.

No. 988-16. The machine gun turret face is missing at the front. Also, there is an entry hole of a hit visible above the red star.

Again, 988-16 a long time after the previous photos, possibly in the autumn of 1941. The tank was moved to the side of the road and all useful parts have been removed. However, the interesting thing with this photo is the German graffiti—'*so endete eine leibe*' (so ends a life). The T-26 model 1939 that was lost with this tank is behind the lorry.

No. 988-17 shortly after it was lost. The main turret is without the antenna. Also, the MG turrets are without amplification.

The Combat Debut of the T-35A Tank in Photos

No. 988-17 after some time has passed. The tank has '*Vorsicht*', which means 'caution', written on the skirt; it was painted over the red star. Interestingly, most of the turrets have not been moved too much, apart from the rear 45-mm gun. From this angle, the damage to the left jack is far more evident, sitting at an angle on the bracket that itself is damaged. The cover for the early exhaust is far more evident in this image; indeed, it was this technical feature that meant it could identified this tank as 899-17 as both of the 988 chassis numbers share this feature.

No. 988-17 from the front. The tank has in fact crashed into a tree. The early driver's vision hatch is clearly visible.

Chassis number 0197-7 at Kubinka.

T-35A 0200-0 was issued to the 68th Tank Regiment in 1941 and was one of four T-45s involved in the Battle of Verba on 30 June 1941. This T-35, as evident by the photographs, was lost in a ditch between two roads that the T-35s were driving up. Due to the locations of the tanks and from combat photographs, 0200-0 was probably in front of 988-16 in the left-hand lane, with 148-39 and 220-27 in the right-hand lane, and 148-30 most likely in front of 220-27.

These tanks were the vanguard of a small group of tanks with a KV-1 and T-26 in the left lane behind 988-16 and two BT-7s behind 220-27 in the right-hand line. The combat photograph suggests that 0200-0 was one of the first causalities of the fighting, possibly fought to a standstill. The post-combat photographs clearly indicate that the tank was hit by many shells. Nos 220-25 and 148-39 were already in flames, having been blown up by air support, with 988-16 rolling past them. The KV-1 is on the road; however, it is not known whether it had turned around yet.

The tank was by far the most popular T-35 to photograph as the tank was at such an interesting angle on the road, with the tank nose first in the ditch that separates the two roads. As time progressed the tanks slowly changed. Notice the condition of the tank and the directions that the turrets are facing. not only indicating that even after the tank fell into the ditch it continued to fight, but this will be used as a rough guide to dating pictures as the turret were moved very occasionally.

T-35A 0200-4

T-35A chassis number 0200-4 was a standard T-35 tank manufactured in 1938 and was the forty-sixth T-35 produced. The technical features include the late exhaust system, late driver's vision hatch, and amplification on the MG turret faces.

Shortly after the battle ended, 30 June 1941. The T-26 is still on the main road, but it too will very shortly be moved to the ditch. It is fair to surmise that the tank was reversing and hit 0200-0 before the crew bailed. The KV-1 is on the left, still on the road before being moved by the Germans. Pay close attention to the position of the turrets. The periscopes are all intact and on the tank and the P-40 AA mount is equipped with its DT-29.

Above: No. 0200-0. A short amount of time after the last picture, probably dating to late July. The tank has had the optics removed, and the T-26 has been moved to the side of the road. There are no fewer than six hits on the tank, including on the barrel of the rear 45-mm gun.

Below: Another view of 0200-0. There is a good view of the T-26 model 1939. Notice the 20-mm thick armour upgrade on the hull and the pressed armour for the gun mantlet. The T-26 also has a slightly different divisional marking. This is probably a different division within the 8th Mechanised Corps, but has the remnants of the white triangle that was painted over or worn off. It is one long line with a very short line above it. The white air identification triangle is painted on the two turret hatches.

A view of 0200-0 with 220-25 at the top of the road and one BT-7 just visible behind the German soldier on the right. It is clear from this picture how deep the tank sunk onto the bank of the drainage ditch. The drainage ditch is still there to this day; however, there is no longer a secondary support road. There are still some remainders from this time with a concrete drainage tunnel in the ditch still there almost eighty years on. It is unknown whether there is anything left buried under the soil from this great battle.

No. 0200-0 from a different angle. The vehicle passing 0200-0 is a Sd.Kfz. 11, which is travelling west, back towards the Ukrainian frontier. The group of soldiers in the road are roughly where T-35 148-39's remains are. It was blown up by air attack, which also appears to have either damaged (or caused the crews to abandon) two BT-7s. It is understandable that these tanks were a spectacle as indicated by the vast amount of photographic evidence of these tanks and the amount of people inspecting them. It is therefore strange that some tanks still remain unaccounted for photographically.

No. 0200-0 now has the front 45-mm gun barrel removed, leaving the sleeve intact. It was probably pushed backwards by the weight of the tank against the bank. The main turret has been rotated to the right, and is a match for the below image. The ball mount in the front MG turret has been removed. Just visible is something written on the side of the skirt, left of the red star.

No. 0200-0 from the front, which gives an interesting view on top of the tank. The P-40 AA mount with the second hatch for the loader is normally obscured. The early driver's access hatch has two separate doors. The front 45-mm gun has been removed. There are two periscope mounts on the turret. This tank has the pressed star on the turret roof, which is between the two periscopes, just visible. This photo offers a glimpse inside the MG turret though the hatch and the front 45-mm turret. The interiors are painted white to utilise what little light is let inside the tank.

Here, the tank has fallen fully into the ditch. This photo possibly dates to early 1942. It is easy to identify this tank as 0200-0 by the fact it is in the ditch and the combat damage it has sustained. The failing condition of the ditch has caused the ditch's side to collapse and allow the tank to fall in. The damage to the rear fender is visible on some photographs of the tank before it fell into the ditch completely. The right-hand side of the track has been completely swallowed by the mud. Interestingly, the rear MG position is open, giving a rather unusual appearance.

No. 0200-0 sits fallen into the ditch as seen from the T-26 tank; this too has fallen into the ditch. There are not many pictures of this T-26 due to the fact that German soldiers preferred to take photographs of the bigger tanks that littered the landscape at Verba. The T-26s replicating systems armour has been removed.

This T-35 was issued to the 68th Tank Regiment and was at the repair centre at Sudova Vyshnia when the war broke. Subsequently, the tank was lost during repairs on 24 June 1941. Outwardly, the tank looks very similar to 148-50, with the same level of repair and the wooden A-frame deployed over the engine deck. However, key differences are the P-40 AA mount and the amplification on the MG turrets. Just like 148-50 and 196-94, this tank was used by German forces for infantry anti-tank training. The tank was subsequently shot at. It is unknown whether the tank was also blown up like 196-94.

T-35A 0200-5

T-35A chassis number 0200-5 was the second to last T-35 produced with the standard hull and cylindrical turrets. It was the forty-seventh T-35A produced. Technical features include the late exhaust and the late driver's vision hatch.

This tank was issued to the 67th Tank Regiment. Shortly after the war started, the tank was given white air identification triangles painted onto the tank. Five white triangles had been painted onto the turret sides. From left to right, there was a triangle on the left next to the main gun and stopping before the pistol port. Another was painted between the two support strips, and the third was directly at the rear of the tank covering the rear MG port. The fourth was on the right between the two support strips and the final one was very small above the cheek MG position. Other triangles on the turret include one on the P-40 AA mount hatch.

No. 0200-4 after capture on 29 June 1941. The M-17L engine is outside the tank. Engine and transmission failures were commonplace for T-35s as the tank was so long that turning caused stress on the latitude and longitude of the tank, the brakes wore out due to the weight of the tank, gearboxes often seized up, and teeth broke. (*Sergey Lotarev*)

Triangles were also painted on the 45-mm gun turret roofs. It is unknown whether more were painted on the turret roof, perhaps over the pressed star on the roof.

The tank was abandoned on the modern T1413 highway, between Zolochiv and Sasiv, close to the village of Yelykhovychi. This is on the outskirts of Zolochiv. The E40 highway is also very close. It is interesting to see how all the tanks were abandoned along the same basic route.

T-35A 0200-9

No. 0200-9 was the last T-35 manufactured with typical turrets before the conical turreted tanks were manufactured. 0200-9 was the forty-seventh T-35 made. This tank's technical features include the late driver's vision hatch, the late exhaust, but most interestingly, the nose of the tank is made of riveted construction rather than of welded construction. This feature is strange among T-35s, with only 196-95 and a conical tank. It is thought they were used to strengthen poor welding.

This tank was lost with the fighting for Sasiv, and was probably the cause of the traffic jam at the choke point seen in the following pictures. According to the losses of the 68th Tank Regiment, 0200-9 broke down then was 'knocked out in action' on 30 June. There is no apparent combat damage to this tank; however, what is evident is that the main turret is facing rearwards, probably engaging a tank.

This tank has actually been viewed by millions of people as it was filmed in the weekly German propaganda film *Die Deutche Wochenschau*, episode 567, 16 July 1941. The tank appears at 26.38, and is initially filmed from the rear, with the commentator saying '*und hier, ein schwerer*

The road from Zolochiv to Sasiv. T-35A 0200-5 sits on the road. It is likely that this tank was driving to Sasiv to engage the Germans there.

The Combat Debut of the T-35A Tank in Photos

No. 0200-5. The tow eye is still intact on the left-hand tow point. Interestingly, there is a good view of all the white triangles on the turrets included on the previous photo. There are five triangles on this tank. There is also a white triangle on the turret P-40 hatch. It is also possible that there is one on the open hatch of the front 45-mm gun turret.

A late photograph of 0200-5, dated 30 April 1942. It had, by this point, spent a whole year sitting in the field. Interestingly, the white triangle is on the turret side. However, the antenna is missing. Note the exhaust pipes under the protective cover, but most interestingly notice the transmission through the missing access hatch. The hinges that the fan cover attaches to and the ladder used to access the fenders are also clearly visible. The troops on the tank appear to be Luftwaffe personnel.

bolschewik panzerkampfwagen...' (and here, a heavy Bolshevik tan...). The film shows this T-35, and T-35A 988-16, with the front of the MG turret face missing and the headlight gone.

The interesting feature with this tank is that it is missing the front left fender up to the second fender-skirt attachment. This is on the left-hand track. This tank was lost on the road from Pisok to Koltiv, on 30 June, close to the village of Ruda-Koltivska. This was all a part of the Sasiv battles.

T-35 234-35

T-35 234-35 was the fiftieth T-35 produced and was the second conical-turreted T-35 to enter production. Like all three of the original production conical T-35s, this machine had a plethora of modernisations added to the tank to improve the lifespan of the tank.

Conical turrets are, of course, the most noticeable update to the tank, with armour that was 30 mm thick on each of the turrets. The hull was moderately redesigned with 30-mm frontal armour that was effectively the bare minimum to even stand a chance on a modern battlefield. The skirts of the tanks were redesigned, becoming shorter to allow the drive wheel to be clear of any obstructions. One major issue with the T-35 was that mud and other debris would build up over the drive wheel and hinder performance.

Along with these changes, access ports were also cut into the skirts, with hinged doors that allowed for access to the rear three bogies of the suspension. Lastly, the access doors for the transmission was redesigned. These new doors were wider and had two handles for removal of the whole panel.

T-35s 234-34, 234-35, and 234-42 were all equipped with the typical clothes-line antennae, which 234-35 still retained in 1941. However, 234-42 had its aerial removed at some point. Unfortunately, there are no pictures of 234-34 currently available; however, it would appear that the tank's gearbox failed while fording a river near Ternopil and was subsequently abandoned by its crew. No. 234-34 served in the 68th Tank Regiment.

No. 234-35 was issued to the 67th Tank Regiment before June 1941 and served in that regiment during the war. However, it was lost due to an unfortunate accident while retreating from Lviv towards Ternopil. The tank crossed a small bridge near the village of Ivanivtsi, which is situated near the town of Stryi. This is actually 70 km south from Lviv, and it would appear that this machine took a different path to other T-35s to reach Ternopil. The tank toppled over, likely due to the bridge collapsing. Photographic evidence suggests that it was almost totally across the bridge before the tank fell. The documentation for the losses of the 67th Tank Regiment describes 234-35's fate as: 'capsized in a river up the tracks in an area with Ivashkovtsy and made unusable 30 June 1941'.

The tank toppled over onto its roof, completely submerging the main turret under the soft mud of the rivers banks and partly submerging the rear of the tank. It is unclear if any crew died; there is no indication that they did as escape hatches are open on the front turrets and the driver's compartment. While difficult, it was possible to move about the interior of a T-35.

Unfortunately, due to the remote location of this tank, not many photographs were taken of the machine; however, Slovakian troops are known to have taken at least four

Above and below: German units try to pass the traffic jab at the choke point of the road. It was a very unlucky for the Soviets to break down here. Opposite, the horse and cart are marching on the grass past the tank.

Below: The traffic jam near Sasiv was caused by a single unreliable tank breaking down, namely T-35A 0200-9. The nose of the T-35 has been reinforced with bolts to support the poor welding of the plates. A Voroshilovets tractor can be seen to the right side of the picture. The T-35 before abandonment was clearly engaging a target as the turret is facing rearward, towards the German tanks.

T-35 234-42

T-35 chassis number 234-42 was the third conical-turreted T-35 produced, the fifty-first T-35 produced, and the second to last T-35 produced in 1938. The term 'T-35A' can be used to denote conical T-35s; however, this specific type of T-35 never had an official name. The T-35B was to be equipped with a V12 diesel engine. A case could be made for using the designation 'T-35C' if the lettering system was being applied; however, from here on, the conical T-35s will be known as T-35s for simplicity.

The tank has an interesting mix of features. Notice that the hull is the same hull used on 196-94 and 196-95 with inspection ports in the skirts. The skirt is the late type, which is missing the last portion that would normally cover the drive wheel. The turret pedestal has the smoke generators homogenous with the pedestal. Most obviously, the turrets are all conical types.

Interestingly, there were multiple types of conical T-35 turrets that retained the basic same shape, whilst cosmetics of the tanks were changed. For example, the main turret of the first two conical turreted T-35s were identical to 234-42's turret, with the exception of the clothes line antenna. No. 744-61 reverted back to the turrets without the antenna, but changed the loader's hatch from a convex-lipped hatch to a concave lid. Then, 744-63 removed the rear ball mount on the turret and changed the loader's access hatch to a 'BT' type hatch.

There were other small changes between conical tanks including the hinges used on the 45-mm gun turrets up to 744-63. No. 234-42's fan cover was the same as the standard production tanks; however, from 234-34 onward, the transmission access hatches were made square with two handles to remove the cover.

T-35 234-42 was issued to the 67th Tank Regiment in June 1941. The tank was abandoned in the tiny village of Zapytiv, Lviv region of Ukraine. The tank lay near the modern Michiel Church (церква Архистратига) on the E40 road. The tank was moved to a drainage ditch which no longer exists, however a black and white railing now stands in its place. The combat records claim the tank was lost on 3 July; however, this is unlikely for the location of the tank. It is far more likely to be 29 or 30 June.

T-35 744-62

T-35 744-62 was built in 1939 and was the fifty-third T-35 produced. Outwardly, this tank looks very similar to 234-42; however, it has some subtle changes. For example, the tank is missing the clothes line antenna, and while not in shot, it has a slightly redesigned secondary turret main turret hatch with a convex lip, rather than a concave one.

This tank is, however, identical to 744-61, which was knocked out in a forest along with 339-30. No. 744-62 was the last T-35 with conical turret with a machine gun in

No. 234-35 on 29 June 1941. This is actually one day before the losses of the 67th Tank Regiment claims that the tank was lost. The author of this image wrote '29 *Juni bei Stryi Galicia*'. This gives historians enough information to locate the tank in the village of Ivanivtsi outside of Stryi, rather than the village of the same name in Ternopil Oblast. In this photograph, the remains of the clothes-line antenna can be seen under the tank next to the smoke generator.

The same tank again. Notice the way the track lays on the running gear. The access ports in the skirts can be clearly observed here.

No. 234-42. The Russians have tried to hide the tank using tree branches, similarly to the unknown T-35. In addition, the armour around the driver's vision hatch is a feature on some cylindrical turreted T-35s, but commonplace on conical T-35s.

the rear of the main turret and a square secondary turret hatch rather than the 'BT' style hatch. In addition, it was the last T-35 conical with the early 45-mm gun turret hatches, with the rivets around the rim of the hatch and the early hinges without the exterior spring.

This tank was issued to the 67th Tank Regiment when war broke out, and was lost in the village of Gorodok. The tank was travelling east, along the modern T1425 road, in the town of Horodok, lviv Oblast. It was originally left standing opposite modern house fifty-nine on the T1425.

T-35 744-63

No. 744-63 was the last T-35 produced with angled inspection ports in the skirt and the last T-35 produced with flat turret pedestal sides. It was manufactured in 1939 and was the fifty-fourth T-35 produced.

Technical features include the late driver's hatch, solid front idler wheel, the 'BT' style secondary turret hatch, and the new exterior spring type turret hatch. This T-35 was a unique type. It was the last tank built with angled hatches on the side skirts, and flat sided

One of the earliest pictures of 234-42, shortly after it was captured by German forces. The tank has tree branches on it to try to hide the tank. The Flak 88 is in the deployed firing position, using the tank as cover.

A slightly blurry photograph of 234-42. The antenna feet on the turret clear denote that this is indeed 234-42.

Sometime between late 1941 and early 1942, the tank was moved right to the side of the road and had its track removed fully. The rear 45-mm gun has had one of the vision ports covered. Also, there is damage to the jack bracket on the turret pedestal.

One of the last photos of 234-42. The track has been removed and moved to the front of the tank. Note the white paint on the fender and wheel to warn German traffic of the hazard. This photo was probably taken in the late autumn of 1941. The child next to the tank gives an interesting sense of scale. The Germans have applied some writing on the smoke generator armour 'property of OKH' which was the 'Oberkommando des Heeres'—otherwise known as the German High Command.

No· 744-62 in the village of Gorodok. Notice that the machine's tow ropes have been deployed.

The photographer from the 257th Infantry Division, after chronicling 715-62 at Sasnow Wisna, moved onto Gorodok. Here, he encountered the conical behemoth that was 744-62. Once again, he put his camera to good use and provided an excellent walkaround of this conical beast. He took the next six photographs; however, these do not have any dates. He does however locate these tanks as Gorodok, which he also noted on 715-61, which is obviously wrong. Here, 744-62 sits shortly after the tank was abandoned, thought to be between 25 and 30 June.

The imposing figure of 744-62. This must have only been a short while after the tank was abandoned as all of the miscellaneous equipment is scattered across the ground. This very quickly was scavenged and either disposed of or used by the Germans.

The right side of the tank. Notice the caps between the hinges in the skirts and the skirt itself as well as the dirt and scrape marks on the skirt and drive wheel. The ladder on the hull side is clearly visible. The pins in the track too are clearly seen, or more correctly not seen, rather buried in each track link. On the inside of the skirt, there can be seen metal guides to help the track and preventing it from sagging too low and catching on the skirt bracket.

The left side of the tank. There are subtle differences to the skirt with a small cut out at the front of the left skirt; it is unknown why this exists, but is on all T-35s. The rear 45-mm gun turret hatch can be inspected with bolts around the hatch edge. The ball mount of the turret had been removed, and now a small window into the tanks turret can be seen. Notice that the turret pedestal is homogenous as in the smoke generators are one with the pedestal rather than being merely attached as an afterthought.

The front of the tank. Notice the driver's vision hatch. These tanks were virtually playgrounds for the German soldiers who found them as is evident in this image.

The rear of the tank and the last of this collection. The fuel can on the ground next to the tank is likely equipment that was stowed on the rear of the tank.

No. 744-62. New transmission hatches were equipped to this tank. Unfortunately, obscured by the German truck, the unknown T-35 with the P-40 AA mount is in front of the building at the end of the road. The ladder issued with the tank is being misused on the side of the tank.

Nineteen soldiers stand on 744-62. There are curious bolts on the front of the fenders.

Another photograph of 744-62. Pay attention to the round shape of the MG position in the turret cheek. The solid turret pedestal is clearly visible in this photograph.

After about eight months sitting in the road, the tank was dragged to the side of the road and the tracks were removed. This image gives an interesting look at the maximum rotation of the rear 45-mm gun. The German car gives an epic sense of scale.

No. 744-62 in mid-1942. Some interesting points on the photo are the missing track, the headlight out of its bracket on the front deck, and the spilled white paint on the smoke generator armour, turret, and side skirt. The soldiers behind the tank are in drill uniform. The tank was moved to the edge of the road and slightly further east down the road. The tank, still on the T1425 road, is opposite the modern building sixty-nine in front of a shop called 'Продукти'—a convenience store—with a sign next to it for a motel in English.

The Combat Debut of the T-35A Tank in Photos 117

No. 744-62 on 7 July 1942. The tank has been moved to the side of the road, tracks have been removed, and the tank has been moved to the side of the road. Take note of the two-piece driver's access hatch.

No. 744-62 with some very important visitors. The turrets are in the same position as the picture on the previous page. There is a Ukrainian child on the gun. These tanks were often used as playgrounds for children. The German officers are of note as they all seem to be high ranking officials—eight men who all seem to be at least offers of rank that would be in commanded of divisions.

No. 744-62 with some very important inspectors. Note the rear turret MG mount and the mount for the aerial. This photo contains two T-35s. The tree on the right of the photo, further down the road, is another T-35 (thought to be 288-43). This is the tank that is in the ditch on page 64. The man on the left is Lt Ferdinand Neuling, the commander of the 239th Infantry Regiment. In the middle is General Hasso von Manteuffel, who was in command of the 7th Panzer Division, which was curiously deployed in Army Group Centre. The general on the right has not been identified.

smoke generators. However, it was the first to be produced without a rear turret MG and a 'BT' style loader's hatch in the turret. In addition, tanks after this were also built with 'BT' style driver's hatches.

This tank served with the 68th Tank Regiment and was one of the last tanks lost. Interestingly, the tank does not have the '=' divisional marking on the turret. As with 744-65/66, it is possible the tank was on loan from the 67th Tank Regiment.

The tank appears to have been abandoned after the flywheel shattered; however, the engine may also have seized. It is curious that the tank is not on the road, rather on the far side of a tree with no hope of ever being on a road again.

Note the white air identification triangles. This tank had three air identification triangles on the turret sides, two either side in-between the two strips of support on the turret, and one huge one at the rear of the turret. In addition, there were white triangles on the 45-mm gun turret hatches.

T-35 744-65/66

This is either T-35 chassis number 744-65 or 744-66; it was either the fifty-seventh or fifty-eighth T-35 produced and either the third or second to last T-35 made.

No. 744-63 stuck at the side of the road. Some evidence suggests that it was originally lost on the road and moved behind the tree.

Note the triangle on the front turret hatch and the flat smoke generator sides. An interesting note is the MG turret inside. While there is no vision port, there is a small slit in the armour. This did not give access to viewing outside of the tank.

While obscured by a tree, 744-63's features are clearly discernible. The reverse of this picture claims 'a 52-ton tank, of the fist great tank battle in Ukraine!' This is obviously describing the counter attack by the red army between 26 June and 1 July 1941.

The last four T-35s—744-64 to 744-67—all shared the basic same features. This included the new side skirts with square access hatches to the suspension, angled smoke generator, turret pedestal armour, 'BT' style hatches for the driver and loader, the exterior spring type 45-mm gun turret hatch, the new shortened rear fan cover, and hinged transmission hatches. However, this tank had the old spider web idler wheels.

Current theories are that this tank was operated by the 67th Tank Regiment, but was on loan to the 68th Tank Regiment, hence the '=' mark on the turret. The tank was lost near the village of Lopuszno, Kremenets district, Ternopil region, on the road to Pochayiv. The closest tank according to the records of being lost was 744-66; however, there is still a chance it could be 744-65 due to the poor documentation.

T-35 744-67
The Last

The last T-35 produced was 744-67. This tank was produced in 1939 and was the fifty-ninth T-35 produced. As with all four of the last production tanks, it features the new side skirts with square access hatches to the suspension, angled smoke generator, turret pedestal armour, 'BT' style hatches for the driver and loader, the exterior spring type 45-mm gun turret hatch, the new shortened rear fan cover, and hinged transmission hatches.

Due to the nature of the photographic record, it is unknown whether this T-35 is 744-65 or 744-66. (*Sergey Lotarev*)

The tank was issued to the 67th Tank Regiment when war broke out. The tank was painted with white aerial identification triangles. There were four on the main turret sides. There were two massive white triangles on either side of the turret with the point roughly at the top of the first support strip. The third one is a massive triangle on the rear of the tank, and the final one is a very small triangle on the cheek machine gun mount. The 45-mm gun turrets also had white triangles that started on the gun mantlets and finished just before the 45-mm gun turret hatches.

This tank was lost in the village of Ozhydiv, travelling west. The records show that the drive shaft snapped. The old highway ran though the village, but the modern E40 highway runs north. The tank sat on the road throughout the rest of the war, slowly degrading, and finally fully dismantled on the roadside. However, the tank was involved in incidents whilst under German occupation. Ukraine was a fairly unwilling province of the USSR. On 30 June 1941, Stepan Bandera, leader of the extreme Ukrainian Liberation Party in Lviv, proclaimed an independent Ukrainian state. He, and his political organization of Ukrainian Nationalists thought that, in their fight against the Soviet Union, they had a powerful ally in Germany. The same was true in other Soviet states. In September 1941, 744-67 had '*слава степанові вандері!*' (English: 'Glory to Stepan Bandera!') written on the skirt and had '*слава украіні!*' ('Glory to Ukraine!') written on the drive wheel. It also had the crest of Ukrainian national party painted on the skirt.

However, the Germans arrested the newly formed Ukrainian government and sent them to concentration camps. Bandera was imprisoned by the Germans until late 1944. Without Bandera present, his extreme political party massacred up to 100,000 Polish civilians in Volhynia and East Galicia in 1943. Stepan Bandera was released in September 1944 and formed the Ukrainian Insurgent Army, which was incorporated into the Wehrmacht. However, this had no major effect on the outcome of the war. Bandera was assassinated in 1959 by the KGB.

The T-35s were quite the playground for curious German soldiers. Here, 744-67 sits as a mere play thing for curious men. The white air identification triangle can be seen on the turret.

No. 744-67 from the front. This photo clearly illustrates the angled smoke generators. This photograph was taken shortly after the tank was abandoned. Unfortunately, the 'BT' style driver's hatch is closed with a German soldier sitting on it. The white air identification triangle is on the turret. Interestingly, there is the same unusual strip of metal hanging of the right-hand jack support that is seen deployed on T-35 234-42. It is still unknown what this was used for.

No. 744-67, again, a very short time after the tank was lost. There are no German warnings on the tank yet and the tracks are complete. Again, notice the angled smoke generator and the white air identification triangles. In this photo, it is possible to make out the 'BT' style driver's access hatch, which was standard issue by this point in production.

No. 744-67 a while into its abandonment. The Germans have painted white warning signs on the tank. The white air identification triangle is on the rear of the turret and on the 'BT' style loader's hatch. There was no identification triangle on the P-40 AA mount, where they were normally painted.

No. 744-67 with 'Glory for Stephen Bandera!' and 'Glory for Ukraine!' written on the skirt and drive wheel. Interestingly, in the old ICM model of a standard production T-35A, it had decals to make this tank. This is bizarre as this tank is a final production T-35, whereas the kit was more akin to 988-16.

This is a very rare photo. This appears to the last confirmed photo of 744-67, possibly in mid-1943. This photo gives an excellent view of the skirt frame on late T-35s. The open transmission hatches were hinged to the tank; this is why the fan cover is so short on these late tanks. The turrets have been removed and how lay in the road. The white paint has survived on his tank for the triangle—there is one on the mantlet of the 45-mm gun turret, and one on each cheek of the turret. Unusually, there does not appear to be one on the P-40 AA mount.

4
Art of the T-35A

Technical Images, Colour Profiles, and Other Information

The maps on pages 129–131 are Polish maps of the Lviv Oblast from the 1930s. The whole area that the T-35s was lost in was originally polish territory before 1939. After the Soviet invasion, the land was 'given' to Ukraine, which at the time was a part of the Soviet Union. The 'marks' on the map indicate tanks lost and their exact location.

T-35A 148-30. Manufactured in 1934 and lost in the defence of Kharkiv, this tank was one of the first production tanks. The antenna was removed, leaving just the feet from the arms. It was upgraded from a six-arm turret to an eight-arm turret, and had a plate welded over the original plate next to the support strip. The tank had an early exhaust.

T-35A 537-70. This tank was lost on the road to Ozhydiv and was manufactured in 1936. Serving in the 67th Tank Regiment, the tank was painted with white air identification triangles on the main turret— one on the inside cheek of the rear 45-mm gun turret and one on the right smoke generator. This picture depicts the tank a short time after capture.

T-35A 988-15. Abandoned in Zolochiv, this T-35 was unique in being the only T-35 with painted numbers on the tank, with this tank being 'fourteen'. Serving in the 67th Tank Regiment, technical features include a complete antenna, unamplified MG faces, and the early exhaust pipe; all are clearly visible in this rendition.

Art of the T-35A

T-35 196-95. Serving in the 67th Tank Regiment and abandoned at the Gorodok repair centre, this tank was one of the hybrid machines that was equipped with an experimental hull that was manufactured in 1937, between batches of regular T-35s. The access panels in the skirt are noticeably larger than those which were implemented onto the later tanks. The front of the tank had a dedication to Lenin, and photographs indicate a small brass Lenin on the smoke generator.

T-35A 0200-0. Knocked out during the Battle of Verba, the tank was one of the vehicles that had the antenna completely removed, leaving just the foot plates. this tank features the '=' mark on the turret from the 68th Tank Regiment. this is perhaps the most 'generic' T-35 depicted in the art, however still an important piece.

T-35A 0200-5. Lost on the road from Zolochiv to Sasiv, this tank served in the 67th Tank Regiment and was covered with white air identification triangles on the turret. Another triangle was at the rear of the turret, and another two were on the right-hand side, with an additional one on the P-40 AA mount hatch.

Above: T-35 234-42. This tank was lost in the village of Zapytiv in the Lviv Oblast. It was the only T-35 conical that was equipped with a clothes line antenna. This was removed, leaving the feet in place. The tank does not have signs of a red star. However, the shirts are covered in mud; therefore, a star has been added for artistic licence. This is another tank from the 67th Tank Regiment.

Below: T-35 744-64. Manufactured in 1939, this tank was lost at the repair centre at Gorodok. It was the first T-35 to be equipped with the square access hatches in the hull. Notice the solid front idler wheel. The smoke generators were angled; however, from this angle, it would not be obvious. This tank was equipped with no markings whatsoever, due to serving in the 67th Tank Regiment.

Opposite above:
1. Unidentified T-35A. The location names on the maps are the original polish names of the villages, however the closest village to the tank was Hamaliivka.
2. T-35A No. 288-11. According to the combat reports of the 68th Tank Regiment, the tank fell from a bridge and caught fire.
3. T-35 No. 234-42. The village that the tank was lost in was Zapytiv. Michiel Church is situated to the east of the tank at the very edge of the village, and the tank was lost further west as the road begins to gently curve.
4. T-35A148-25. The brewery is at the next junction to the east.
5. T-35A chassis number 228-14. The village that is directly to the south is Staryi Yarychiv. Following the road further east if found the village of Banyunyn, where 288-65 is found.

Opposite below:
This map is of the Zolochiv Oblast. This was roughly 70 km away from Lviv.
1. T-35A No. 988-15. The tank was lost next to the old cemetery.
2. On the Zolochiv-Sasow highway is T-35A No. 0200-5.
3. Two T-35s were lost to the east of Sasiv, the southernmost tank being T-35A 148-22.
4. T-35A No. 0200-9.
5. Bilyi Kamin, which is the location of T-35A No. 183-3. The tank was lost in a junction in the village about 50 m away from the Zolochiv road.
6. T-35A No. 537-70. The tank was on the road from Ozhydiv to Yosypivka.

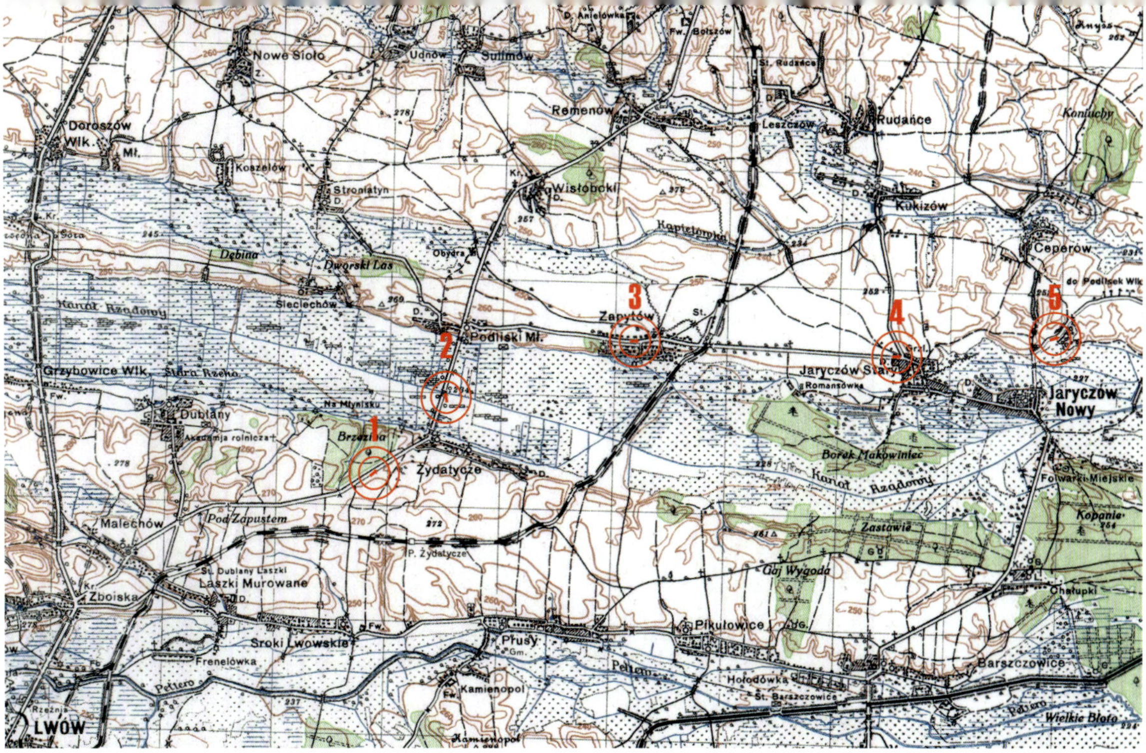

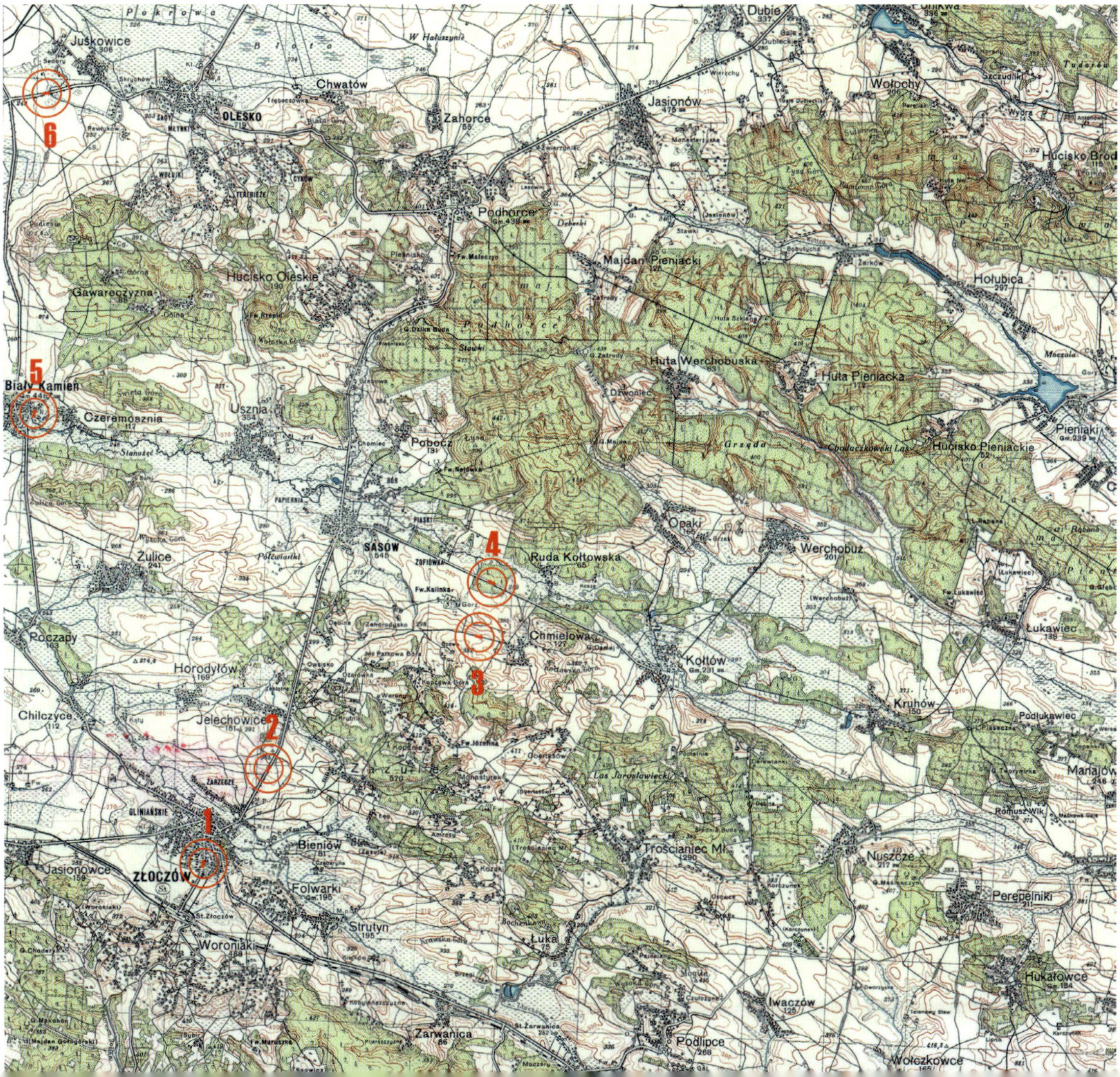

Above:

Sadova Vyshnia (*Sadowa Wisznia*), the repair centre for the 68th Tank Regiment. The repair centre was roughly in the centre of the village, marked on the map by the three T-35s deployed there.
1. T-35A 148-50 situated in the repair centre at Sadova Vyshnia.
2. T-35A chassis number 196-94.
3. T-35A 0200-4.

The other T-35 in Sadova Vyshnia was 715-61. The exact location of the tank has unfortunately not been found.

Below:

Gorodok, the repair centre of the 67th Tank Regiment. In all, seven T-35s were lost in Gorodok.
1 and 2. On the main road heading towards Lvov, two tanks were lost. 1 is T-35 chassis number 744-62 and 2 is an unknown T-35A. Both tanks were heading east towards Lviv.
3. Likely 220-27.
4. Likely 537-80.
5. T-35A 196-95.
6. T-35A 744-64.
7. T-35A 339-75.

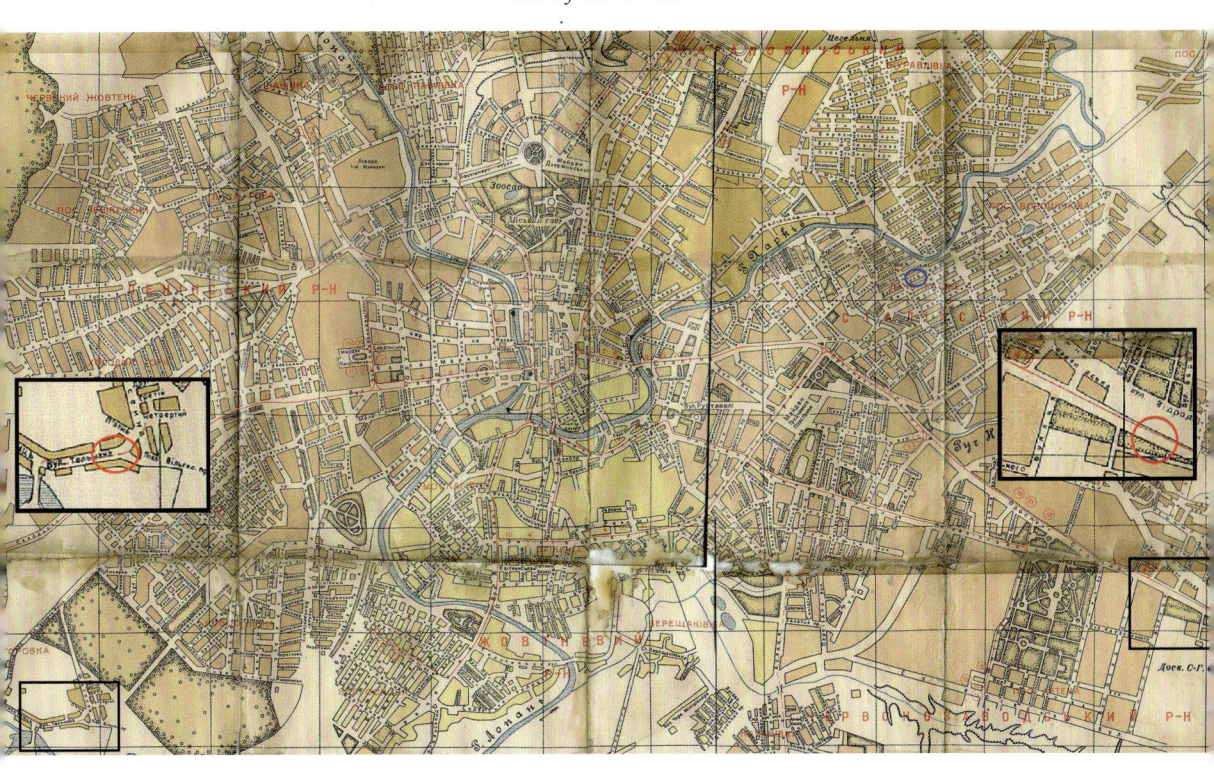

A map of Kharkiv from 1938. The layout of the city is vastly different from today, as the city was annihilated from the fighting between 1941 and 1943. The location of 220-28 is now a small wooded area in the eastern approaches to the city (the right-hand box). On this map, we can see a close up of Stalin Prospekt on the east side of the city. A short way down from 'Zelenyy Gay' park, there are some political buildings. The tank was laid up here. The 'Zelenyy Gay' ('Зелений Гай') park still exists, however the road layout has vastly changed. The location of 148-30 was in the west of the city (the left-hand box). The current location of this tank would be Barkalova Street, about 40 m west of the Karkiv Professional College, opposite Building 14 (ХАРЬКОВСКИЙ ПРОФЕССИОНАЛЬНЫЙ ЛИЦЕЙ'). The blue circle in the east of the city, is where the tank 537-90 was destroyed by its crew. This tank was the last single hatch T-35 built.

5

Tanks that Served Alongside T-35 Tanks

T-35 tanks were not alone in battle. Many other tanks served alongside both in combat and in their abandonment. The 67th and 68th Tank Regiments were not only equipped with T-35s—they also fielded BTs, T-26s, and even some flame-throwing tanks. Other regiments with various tanks also fought alongside the 67th and 68th; one example is a KV-1 lost at Verba, which belonged to another regiment in the 34th Tank Division.

A breakdown of the 68th Tank Regiment's structure describes a full complement of thirty-eight T-35s, of which thirty were deployed. Unfortunately, it is likely that this fails to account for tanks in training schools and tanks going though capital rebuilds. Between the 67th and 68th, a total of eleven tanks listed in inventories were, in fact, not deployed in combat.

Flame-throwing Tanks

Included in the 68th's breakdown were three flamethrower-variant T-26s. Two of these have been identified through post-combat photographs as KhT-26s—essentially T-26 M1931s with one sub-turret removed, the DT ball mount offset to one side, and a long flamethrower inserted next to it. These can be indeed attributed to the 68th due to their '=' divisional markings on the turret.

BTs

The well-known BT tanks that were lost at the Battle of Verba belonged to the reconnaissance unit with the 67th.

The 68th was also equipped with BT tanks. When it was at full strength, it had eleven in its ranks. However, it is unknown whether or not these were given the '=' divisional marking. This therefore makes it hard to identify these BTs through photographs, and thus, it is unknown whether or not they were sent into combat with T-35s.

T-26s

At peak strength, the 68th Tank Regiment had eighteen T-26 tanks. There is evidence to suggest that these T-26s were given the '=' divisional marking. One photograph in particular shows two T-26 Model 1939s with these markings. It is unknown exactly where these T-26s were lost, but there are no photographs indicating the tanks were lost physically alongside T-35s.

The T-26s that served at the Battle of Verba belonged to a different regiment within the 34th Tank Division. There were two T-26s lost in the battle, both tanks Model 1939s. The more famously documented was the Model 1939 lost alongside 0200-0. It would appear that the tank reversed into 0200-0 before being abandoned by its crew. No evidence of combat damage exists on the tank, apart from one small hole on the fender. The other T-26 Model 1939 was lost the other side of Verba along with 988-16. There is, again, no evidence that the tank was hit; however, photographic evidence of this tank is lacking.

T-34

While no T-34s were deployed or lost next to T-35s, they were certainly available at the time. Of course, the T-34 needs no introduction as one of history's greatest machines ever manufactured. Note should be made that one T-35 deployed at Moscow was deployed with T-34s; photos exist of this tank with a T-34 in Moscow.

T-28

Only one T-28 has been found alongside a T-35 tank. The tank in question belonged to the 10th Tank Division of the 15th Mechanised Corps. The tank was abandoned in Zolochiv with T-35A 988-15. Originally, the tank was lost about 50 m down the road from 988-15; however, the two tanks were moved together with their tracks removed. The T-28 in question was a Model 1936 with a P-40 AA mount updated with additional plates.

The KOVO (Kiev Special Military District) deployed 208 T-28 tanks alongside the T-35s with the 34th Tank Division. All were lost between June and October. All T-35s were lost between June and July.

KV-1 and KV-2s

One KV-1 served at Verba and was a part of a separate tank division within the 34th Tank Division. Interestingly, the tank is found in the ditch between the two roads at Verba facing the wrong way. The damage clearly depicts that it was heavily under fire and was possibly the last tank lost. The knockout blow was at the rear.

There was also a KV-2 that served at Zolochiv, and was lost in the village with T-35 988-15. It is unknown what division it belonged to; however, the tank was abandoned in the village of Zolochiv on the other side of the valley that the village sits in.

A HT-26 flame-throwing tank that belonged to the 68th Tank Regiment.

A T-26 Model 1940 attached to the 68th Tank Regiment. All of the regiment's T-26s were lost away from T-35s.

The T-26 that was lost at Verba on 30 June 1941. Take note of the distinctive turret markings on the tank; there was a white triangle that was painted over and had a white line painted across it. However, remains of the white triangle can be seen.

While this T-26 was not lost with a T-35, it is clearly from the same regiment as the T-26 that was lost at Verba. Readers with a keen eye will notice the subtle differences between the two tanks. This tank, for example, had two periscopes and was also equipped with a radio.

Left: The T-28 lost in Zolochiv alongside 988-15.

Below: The KV-1 lost alongside the T-35s at Verba. Notice that this tank is covered with white air identification triangles.

T-37As

The 67th is believed to have had roughly ten T-37A light amphibious tanks deployed in their reconnaissance unit. All of these vehicles were abandoned in Gorodok in 1941. They were abandoned in the repair centre, in front of the T-35s being repaired.

The Engagement at Sasiv

One other engagement that involved a T-35 was the withdrawal from the small town of Sasiv. There was a brief spat between retreating Soviet forces and advancing German forces, in which a KV-2, three KV-1s, a T-40, and several BT-7s were lost, along with an unknown T-35.

T-27s

These small tankettes were designed from a Vickers Tankette. The crew of two consisted of a driver and a machine gunner. The 67th Tank Regiment fielded a number of these tanks, all of which were abandoned at Gorodok.

HTZ-16 'Tractor Tanks'

Four T-35s were deployed in Kharkiv in October with the Separate Armoured (anti-tank) Unit. Within this unit, the T-35s served with thirteen HTZ-16s. These tractor tanks, or self-propelled guns, were one of the most interesting yet mysterious tanks that served alongside T-35 tanks; in fact, they were also the most numerous.

These assault guns were manufactured at the Kharkiv-based Tractor Works, a separate factory to the KhPZ. They were essentially STZ-3 chassis that incorporated elements of the STZ-5 tractor, with 20-mm plates attached to this and a 45-mm gun. Around 1,600 chassis were manufactured, but no more than 113 were fielded due to the evacuation of the factory. The remaining chassis were used by the Germans, who continued STZ-3 production at HTZ.

A T-27 abandoned at the Gorodok repair centre. T-35 196-95 can be seen behind.

A HTZ-16 tank. These machines served alongside T-35s in Kharkov in October 1941.

6

Reviewing the Performance of the T-35A

As this book has proved, the T-35 was not renowned for its combat abilities, nor was it the basis for future tank developments (aside from the short-lived SU-14 self-propelled gun project). In order to understand why the T-35 was such a failure, five sets of problems must be assessed—design phase; production issues; mechanical issues; crew issues; and overall conceptual issues.

Reliability and Manoeuvrability

Perhaps the most obvious flaw of the T-35 was its sheer dimensions. The prototype's huge size meant that there were a variety of mechanical issues that needed ironing out before the general T-35 concept could even be considered a viable design. For example, its length meant that the engine, transmission, gearbox, and drive shaft were all put under huge stress, which often lead to breakdowns and mechanical failures. These issues were supposed to have been solved in the T-35A production model, but the tank still clearly suffered. Of the fifty-two tanks recorded in the losses of the 68th and 67th Tank Regiments, along with the one other known tanks fielded at Kharkiv, twenty-six were lost due to mechanical failure.

The T-35 also suffered from its size in other ways. The high silhouette of the tank was a significant disadvantage. The tanks were easy targets for enemy tanks, AT guns, and aircraft (such as at the Battle of Verba). Also, any possible advantage of stealth would have also been lost due to the T-35 being so conspicuous.

Another point about size concerns the tank's weight—with such large dimensions comes such a large weight, and the tank's weight proved to hinder its manoeuvrability. It simply proved to be too heavy for the unsophisticated road infrastructure of Ukraine, leading to many tanks being bogged down. Bridges also caused the T-35 problems. It is known that two T-35s fell from bridges in unknown circumstances. However, it can be assumed that this was due to either driver error (deriving from poor training) or the tanks simply being too wide for the bridge and falling off as a result.

Poor Soviet Industry

These inherent shortcomings of the tank were also compounded by the fairly poor manufacturing capabilities of Soviet industry. When the tanks were ordered, Soviet industry was primitive compared to other nations, and it was still experiencing its modernisation under Stalin. Therefore, for the USSR, it was more than a goliath task to produce these goliath tanks. The factories had no experience whatsoever with the manufacture of a machine as complex as the T-35. As a result, many parts were rejected; many more parts were flawed, which were consistently low quality.

Issues with poor manufacturing could come in a variety of forms. For example, in 1936, there was a major issue with the manufacture of the plates that were made for the hulls of the tanks. Rather than being 20-mm thick, they were actually made 23-mm thick, and it was not until the plates were attached to the tank that this flaw was discovered. Rather than starting afresh, the engineers decided to keep the defective plates. This not only added too much weight for the already stressed engine, but buckled the chassis of the tanks. Such a small error margin should indicate the precision required in the manufacture of such a complex tank; precision was not necessarily available to Soviet industry.

As if the manufacture of the tank was not plagued enough, Soviet engineers were often purged while they were trying to improve the tanks. It is a sad fact that many talented men were killed off on the simple accusation of treason. For example, engineer and designer Andrykhvich (who was working on improving the already abysmal gear box) was arrested and shot in 1935 for being 'an enemy of the people'; needless to say, this was likely a false accusation. It is therefore no wonder that almost 50 per cent of T-35s broke down due to gearbox failure. In fact, this gearbox issue was not exclusive to the T-35, with many other Soviet tanks (such as the T-34) succumbing to mechanical failure due to poor manufacturing. Thus, aforementioned technical errors have something to do not just with the poor quality of Soviet industry, but avoidable design flaws which were only left unresolved because of Stalin's purges, which involved some of the USSR's top engineers.

Crew Issues

To say that the T-35 suffered from its designers would be totally unfair as it also suffered partly from the limitations of its crews. As mentioned earlier, the driver had a huge task of driving such a large tank, which clearly led to driver-related losses of at least two tanks, but this was perhaps the least important of crew problems. Moreover, if the tank were to make it to combat, then the tank also suffered as a result of the limitations of its commander.

It was found that a multi-turret tank commander could not successfully co-ordinate the gun turrets of the tank to effectively engage the enemy. In the heat of battle, with numerous enemy tanks and AT guns to face off against, having all guns firing at their optimum rate would be, for obvious reasons, desirable if not necessary. If the tank's concept was the intention to move around eight guns on one platform and use them to similar effect as if they were on separate tanks, then this was, clearly, an impossibility. Thus, if the T-35 was not able to give optimum combat use for its guns, it could not, by extension, give optimum combat use for its trained crews. These trained crews might be better used in conventional tanks such as the T-34, KV-1, or even the T-26, in order perform to their optimum.

Leaving aside the idea of crews performing to some kind of abstract notion of an optimum use, the crews had other issues with the T-35. The design of the tank often put the crew's safety at risk. When certain turrets were rotated into certain positions, their bustles or overhang often covered the escape hatches for crewmen in different sections of the tank. This was such an issue that the interior of the T-35 had a complex lighting system to warn crew when they were obstructing hatches. This poorly designed escape hatch system meant that T-35 crews were more likely to die in combat, and thus could not escape to crew another vehicle, and fight another day.

The layout of the turrets was not just an issue for the crew's safety, but was also a major issue for the tank's combat capabilities. Already mentioned was the issue of coordinating the tank's many turrets, but compounding this fact were the turret's own limitations. The arrangement of turrets meant that no more than one turret (in this case, the 76-mm main turret) could have had a 360-degree turning angle. Thus, if the T-35 were to engage an enemy tank, it could (if engaging at an angle) only fire one 45-mm gun and the 76-mm gun to hit the enemy tank. The other 45-mm gun could, in theory, track the enemy tank (if either vehicle were to be moving) and then engage once the tank has moved into its sights, and out of the other 45-mm gun's sights.

This would sound like a non-issue as two turrets from a single tank facing the enemy was actually a mathematical improvement on the usual one gun from a single tank. However, the issue of coordinating and issuing orders to the turrets is still an issue that brings the supposed benefit of two or more guns on one vehicle into question.

Consider also that if the 76-mm and the 45-mm guns were installed on a T-28, and two T-26s respectively, then all guns could, in theory, at all times be facing the enemy tank. However, it would be somewhat naïve to suggest that fielding multiple tanks would be a comprehensive improvement on a T-35. With regards to coordination, due to the fact that Soviet tanks typically did not have radio sets (with the exception of scarce command tanks) and rather relied on flag semaphore, having a mixture of tanks would suffer from the same, if not, worse lack of co-ordination as a single T-35.

Despite this, the fact still remains that the T-35 having multiple turrets (which, by nature, do not give a wide enough traverse arc) is a significant design failure. At best, the guns are not being used to their full potential, and at worst, attempting to coordinate the vehicle's many guns could lead to the tank being knocked out.

The Red Army

With a lot of blame for the tank's failure firmly resting on its mechanical issues, physical limitations, and crew limitations, some consideration must be given to the overall state of the Red Army. In fact, it is the poor state of the Red Army that ultimately caused the T-35 to perform so poorly in combat.

The Red Army in 1941 was one that was poorly trained and was only just learning the lessons of the Spanish Civil War and the Winter War. Stalin's bloody purges of the 1930s had effectively wiped out the officer corps, leaving limp-wristed political commissars with no combat experience thus taking command of units. This led to many poor military decisions that cost the lives of many millions of soldiers. For example, at the engagement at Sasiv, the officers in charge of the retreating Soviet forces failed to deploy a rear guard to cover the retreat of the Soviet armoured force. This led to many needless loss of vehicles (including two T-35s: 0200-9 and 148-22) and men, effectively throwing away a strategic reserve and leading to further losses.

It was also typical that crews of tanks were not only improperly trained on their respective tanks, but often not taught the basics of tank warfare. An inherent issue of the Red Army was the lack of training with regards to defence. This issue stemmed back to Stalin, with his vision that any war conducted by the Red Army would be one where the USSR was the aggressor. Notably, it was in fact this policy that Hitler used as an excuse to attack the Soviet Union. Without the Red Army capable of defending itself effectively, the USSR handed the Wehrmacht the initiative, and threw away any chance of a coherent defence that could have stopped the Wehrmacht earlier than at the gates of Moscow. By not learning the vital concepts of defence, many tanks (including almost every single T-35) were needlessly lost during the panicked retreat in the summer of 1941.

Similarly, often was the case that in an assault, the fast light tanks (such as the BT-7 and T-50) would advance at such a rapid rate that they would leave the heavy tanks (such as the T-35 and KV-1) behind. These light tanks would therefore not have any heavy tank support when engaging an enemy and would be destroyed and lost. This would then leave the heavy tanks to fight alone, and often were picked off one by one, rather than having the support of the light tanks to keep enemy gunners confused and overwhelmed. Thus, scores of tanks could be lost in an otherwise favourable assault, simply due to their lack of tactical coordination and awareness. Indeed, this relates not only to the general lack of radios in Soviet tanks, but also poor training of crews for tank combat and the lack of experience by Soviet officers in organising an assault.

In addition to being poorly trained and commanded, these tank units were ineffectively equipped with regards to tools necessary to keep the T-35s operational. These tools include ammunition, prime movers, and other support vehicles. Some regiments were also inefficiently equipped with too many different types of tanks.

The 68th Tank Regiment, for example, fielded no less than four different types of tanks that all required their own spare parts, recovery vehicles, ammunition, and even fuel. At peak, the regiment fielded thirty T-35s, 16 T-26s, 12 BT-7s, and three flame-throwing KHT-26s. Each vehicle needed specific parts for engines, transmissions, and running gears for their maintenance. Worse still, some of the engines used by these tanks were diesel, and others were petrol, and therefore needed separate refuelling trucks. No doubt, the need for different munitions, parts, and even fuel would cause a logistical nightmare. With its poor organisation, the Red Army could simply not provide all of these vital supplies, leading to some vehicles not being fit for service.

Prime movers were also a major issue in the Red Army. When it came to tanks, these were vehicles, typically tractors, which acted as recovery vehicles. However, the Red Army did not field enough prime movers in the recovery role, because they had to, instead, deploy them in the role of heavy gun towing because they lacked sufficient gun towing vehicles. Indeed, it is no myth that the Red Army was in dire need of mechanisation in the late 1930s and early 1940s. To make matters worse, the T-35 required the heaviest tractors to tow the tank if it broke down or got bogged down, and these could not always be provided.

This clear inability to efficiently run a division lead to many tanks breaking down and not being able to be successfully recovered. In effect, they were lost only due to cripplingly poor organisational and logistical decisions taken by Stalin's 'limp-wristed political commissars'.

Considering maintenance further, T-35s also required much more maintenance than conventional contemporary tanks. Due to the previously discussed length and weight of the tank, many parts were over worked or stressed. Such parts as the engine, transmission, drive shaft, and gear box were overworked, and the vehicle was often poorly driven, leading to a high malfunction rate. Another point to note is that the sheer volume of the tank meant that, by definition, the amount of time spent repairing the tank was increased. Comparing the amount of maintenance of a T-26 needs to a T-35, it is clear that the T-35 would have spent less time engaging the enemy than the T-26, reducing its combat effectiveness.

All in all, the T-35's poor performance was not simply an issue with the design and concept. It is clear that other factors such as inferior manufacturing techniques, and poor crew training had huge impacts of the T-35's ultimate combat value. However, this is clearly not the full story. There were huge losses for all types of Soviet tanks that were deployed in 1941. The losses were absolutely staggering, with no major discretion to the individual qualities and merits of respective models (perhaps with the exception of the off KV tank).

This, again, comes down to poor deployment of tanks, poor organisation of regiments, and poor organisation of the Soviet defence. The only blame for this can be attributed to the Red Army's leadership; after all, they are the ones that decided how crews are trained, how tank regiments were organised, and how the tanks were deployed in combat. As mentioned, the officer corps of the Red Army was decimated by Stalin's purges, thus meaning that inexperienced junior officers became general staff and, perhaps, by a long extension of circumstances, it does not seem unreasonable to suggest that Stalin was to blame for the abysmal combat debut of the T-35. Stalin's purges targeted Soviet engineers, and perhaps without the death of engineer and designer Andrykhvich, the T-35 would have had its gearbox issues resolved, but the quality of Soviet tanks did not matter in 1941; only their deployment did. Even with the T-35's inherent design flaws, without Stalin's purges, the Red Army would have a significantly more effective officer's corps, which would surely have made the Red Army a more effective defensive force in 1941.

Sources and Further Reading

Books

Baryatinskiy, M., *T-34 Medium Tank 1939-1943* (Ian Allan Publishing: 2007)
Kinner, J., *Land Battleship: The Russian T-35 Heavy Tank* (Barbarossa Books: 2000)
Kinner, J., *Steel Fortress T-28 Medium Tank* (Barbarossa Books: 2000)
Porter, D., *Soviet Tank Units 1939-1945* (Amber Books Ltd: 2009)

Reference of T-35 Photos and Chassis Numbers

t35incombat.narod.ru/index.htm
grayknight.narod.ru/T-35/T-35.htm

Table of Production

t35incombat.narod.ru/serial.htm

Online Sources

commons.wikimedia.org/wiki/File:Map_of_Kharkov_(1938).jpg
tanks-encyclopedia.com/ww2/soviet/soviet_T-35.php
aviarmor.net/tww2/tanks/ussr/

Table of Losses

t35incombat.narod.ru/images/act-67-1.jpg
t35incombat.narod.ru/images/act-67-2.jpg
t35incombat.narod.ru/images/act-68-1.jpg
t35incombat.narod.ru/images/act-68-2.jpg